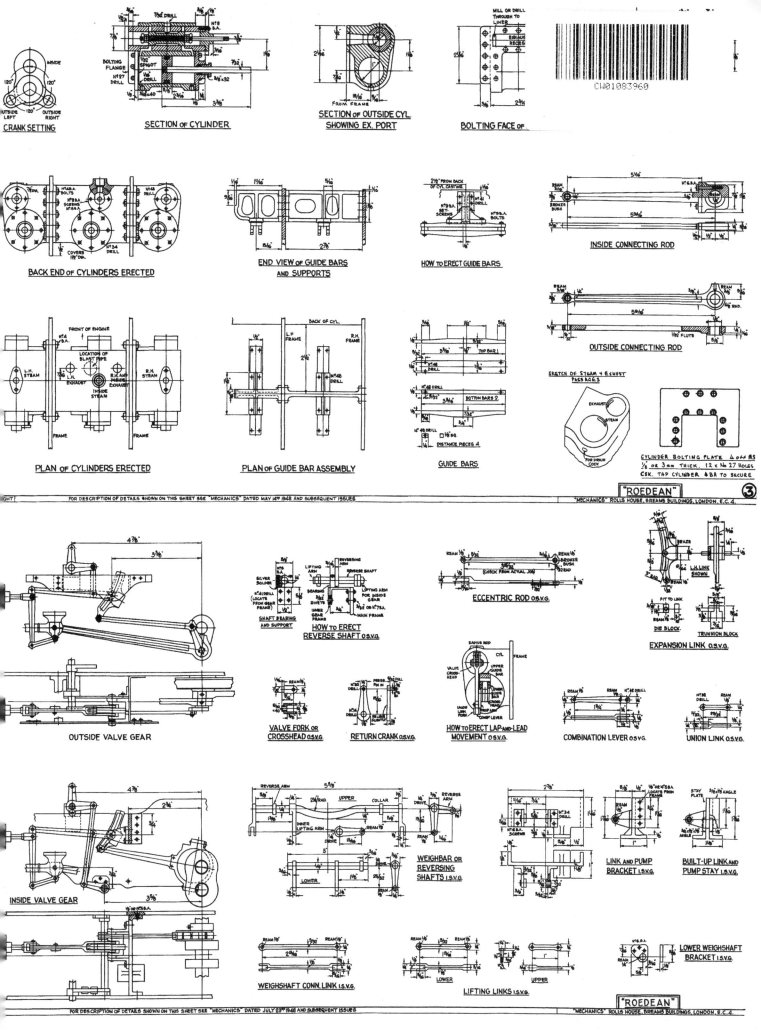

CRANK SETTING

SECTION OF CYLINDER

SECTION OF OUTSIDE CYL. SHOWING EX. PORT

BOLTING FACE OF

BACK END OF CYLINDERS ERECTED

END VIEW OF GUIDE BARS AND SUPPORTS

HOW TO ERECT GUIDE BARS

INSIDE CONNECTING ROD

PLAN OF CYLINDERS ERECTED

PLAN OF GUIDE BAR ASSEMBLY

GUIDE BARS

OUTSIDE CONNECTING ROD

SKETCH OF STEAM & EXHAUST PASSAGES

CYLINDER BOLTING PLATE 4 OFF MS $\frac{1}{8}$ OR 3mm THICK, 12 x No 27 HOLES CSK. TAP CYLINDER 4 BA TO SECURE

"ROEDEAN"

③

OUTSIDE VALVE GEAR

SHAFT BEARING AND SUPPORT

HOW TO ERECT REVERSE SHAFT O.S.V.G.

ECCENTRIC ROD O.S.V.G.

EXPANSION LINK O.S.V.G.

L.H. LINK SHOWN

DIE BLOCK.

TRUNNION BLOCK

VALVE FORK OR CROSSHEAD O.S.V.G.

RETURN CRANK O.S.V.G.

HOW TO ERECT LAP-AND-LEAD MOVEMENT O.S.V.G.

COMBINATION LEVER O.S.V.G.

UNION LINK O.S.V.G.

INSIDE VALVE GEAR

WEIGHBAR OR REVERSING SHAFTS I.S.V.G.

LINK AND PUMP BRACKET I.S.V.G.

BUILT-UP LINK AND PUMP STAY I.S.V.G.

WEIGHSHAFT CONN. LINK I.S.V.G.

LIFTING LINKS I.S.V.G.

LOWER WEIGHSHAFT BRACKET I.S.V.G.

"ROEDEAN"

'LBSC' at Norbury in the 1920s.

'LBSC'- HIS LIFE AND LOCOMOTIVES
Memorial Edition

*A Pictorial Appreciation
and Biography of
Lillian ('Curly') Lawrence, AMI.LOCO.E.*

by Brian Hollingsworth

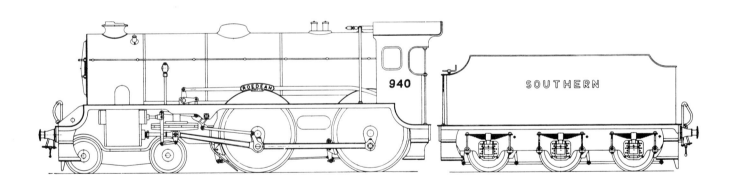

ROEDEAN was a design for a 3½" gauge Southern Railway Schools class 4-4-0, published in Mechanics. It was typical of Curly that he tried to put right the fact that no girls' schools were included amongst the prototypes' names. There was also a Gauge 1 version called Girton.

© The Estate of Brian Hollingsworth 2003

British Library Cataloguing-in Publication-Data: a catalogue record of this book is held by the British Library.

ISBN No. 0-9536523-5-1

First Printing 1982 by Croesor Junction Press

Second Printing 2003 by
Camden Miniature Steam Services
Barrow Farm, Rode, Frome, Somerset. BA11 6PS

First printing typeset by Oxford Publishing Co. Limited

Second printing layout prepared by Salisbury Printing & Camden Studios.

Printed and Bound by Biddles Ltd. Guildford & Kings Lynn

Camden stock one of the widest selections of engineering, technical and transportation book to be found.
Write to the above address for a copy of their latest Booklist.

The front end-paper is decorated by a selection from the construction drawings for ROEDEAN, *obtainable from Reeves 2000.*

Acknowledgements (First Printing)

First, my most grateful thanks are due to Mavis Harriott Curly's literary executor, for allowing me to interview her, to see many mementoes, and to use so much of Curly's papers, drawings and writing in this book. Similar gratitude is due to Mr. Gospatric Home, Managing Director of the Model and Aeronautical Press, without whose permission to use material from the *Model Engineer* this book could never have existed. A. J. Reeves & Co., suppliers for so long of castings, drawings and materials for 'LBSC' locomotives have also been generous in allowing me to use the designs from English Mechanics to illustrate the book. The extract and drawing from the U.S. magazine *Modelmaker* (now incorporated in *Railroad Model Craftsman*) in chapter 6 appears by kind permission of Harold Carstens of Carstens Publications Inc.

Curly's friends from amongst the Model Engineering fraternity both here and across the Atlantic have also been generous with their time and trouble to tell me as much as they knew about someone who meant a great deal to them: Tom Glazebrook, Geoffrey Cashmore, George Barlow, Carl Purinton, Charles Small, Geoffrey Smith, Maisie Frost, George Murray, Edwin Fox, John Clancey, Laurie Lawrence, Dennis Craddock, F. A. Abbott, Geoffrey Randell, Robin Davies and Don Young.

Many others who never knew Curly but still considered themselves to be his admirers also responded with facts, photographs and other help: Keith Wilson, Glyn Dando, Paul Reise, Bobby Jones, Alec Farmer, David Piddington, Neil Simkins. In view of past events, I particularly appreciate the help given by Ernest Steel and his wife Eleanora (nee Greenly). Particular mention must be made of some medical advice given to me by Dr. Brian Rogers and, finally, my special thanks to Margot Cooper who typed the manuscript and to my wife Everil who corrected the proofs.

Acknowledgements (Second Printing)

The first printing of this book was, effectively, a memorial to its subject - this second printing fulfils the same function, but is intended also as a memorial to Brian Hollingsworth, a man who, like 'LBSC', loved railways, and especially the steam locomotive.

The publisher of this printing would like to offer special thanks to, firstly, Mrs Everil Hollingsworth for her gracious permission to reprint, and, secondly, to Dr. Brian Rogers for his Appreciation of Brian Hollingsworth.

Considerable additional help was provided by Keith Humphreys, Bob Jones, George Barlow, Geoff Stait and Bob Shephard to whom grateful thanks are also extended.

Brian Hollingsworth
(1923 - 2001)
An Appreciation

Brian Hollingsworth died on 23rd December 2001, aged 78; he had been unwell for several years following a stroke. I first met him at the meeting in Birmingham called to discuss the formation of a Society for those active or interested in Miniature Railways. The date was 1975, and the 7¼" Gauge Society, specifically for that gauge, had been formed the previous year. This second Society, however, had a more general objective - to include 7¼" and upwards to the larger gauges.

Brian was one of the movers of the meeting, and became a founder member, committee man and Vice President of what was called the *Heywood Society* - a title recalling Sir Arthur Heywood, the father of such railways.

Brian was memorable as a tall, courteous, generous man of many talents, and for the gift of friendship, to say nothing of his encyclopedic knowledge on railway matters.

In 1929 he was given a present of a book, which probably set the pattern of his life, called "The Dreamland Express"; this told the story of three boys who came across a steam locomotive in a wood, and went on to describe their adventures on the engine to reach "the end of the world". The original book had been carefully preserved to be read to his children, and as Brian had four children, and there was only one book, he sought out the holder of the copyright in America and obtained enthusiastic encouragement to reprint, which he did from his own *Croesor Junction Press*. The original edition of this book was also published "in house", while Brian continued to write a range of books in his cosy retreat in North Wales; his books were notable for their meticulous research and excellent prose, and covered a range of topics including Standard Gauge as well as Narrow Gauge and Atlases of World Railways and Train Travel.

In the sad days of the demise of steam Brian, and others, pioneered the preservation of redundant steam locomotives, and he became the owner of an ex L.M.S. Black 5 4-6-0, now resident on the North Yorkshire Moors Railway, and named "Eric Treacy", and he had shares in others.

In 1978 Brian, in association with "Ffestiniog Travel", led a group of twenty six enthusiasts to India: we crossed India, including Delhi, Agra, and thence to Darjeeling, and south to Ootacamund in the South-West. There were tour guides wherever we went, but the knowledge about Indian Railways and locomotives came from Brian's retentive memory.

Whatever the problems were, the unflappable Hollingsworth was master of the situation, calmly assessing the problem and soothing ragged nerves, often with a joke told with a wide smile.

In 1984, a smaller party of eight headed for India again; two weeks before our departure the Indian Prime Minister Mrs. Ghandi was assassinated. Political problems threatened to upset the tour, but it was all smoothed out, and again we had a memorable experience.

When he moved to North Wales Brian had offered his help as a Civil Engineer to the Ffestiniog Railway, and enjoyed the days inspecting this line, of which he held a high opinion.

When he had settled into his home he planned a 7¼" gauge Railway of heroic proportions. The site was a narrow valley, rising rapidly from the road up a narrow track to the house, some 80 ft. above, the only flat areas being near the main road, and about 15 ft. above the house chimney. Only a Civil Engineer could have considered this a practical idea, and only by using the methods used on the Darjeeling Himalayan Railway could it be countenanced. Brian set about building curved bridges, and with these formed spirals so that two loops could be fitted across the valley. The bridges were constructed in timber and he calculated the dimensions of their component parts with the position of all bolt holes and submitted the designs to the Jarrah Importing Co. in London, where they were machined and drilled. When delivered, he spent a happy summer erecting them. To the casual onlooker, the result appeared rather spidery for the large locomotives he planned to use, but to the end they did not fail. He had been slowly collecting engines, all 7¼" gauge. A Darjeeling B Class Tank, a Rio Grande 2-8-0 & 2-8-2, an East African

Class 59 Garrett, an electric Swiss "Crocodile", etc. It was unfortunate that, before completion of the railway, his health began to decline, but he had helpers skilled enough to finish the project. At last it was completed, and the *Heywood Society* were invited to a great opening; alas the monsoon arrived and although many locomotives and trains moved, it was really a severe disappointment.

Within a month of this opening Brian sustained a stroke, and was forced to move from the inaccessible house, the railway being dismantled and disposed of. The locomotives found good homes, and the track is being used again to build elsewhere.

Brian became very frail in his last years, and found getting about a problem. His mind, however, remained unimpaired until his death, and we were able to take him out on railway orientated trips, keeping him in touch with the interests to which he had contributed so much.

He is much missed, and this, and his other books, are his memorial.

Dr. Brian Rogers
January 2003

A rare picture of Curly (in beret) driving a visiting locomotive on his track at Purley Oaks, Surrey.

THE OLD ENGINE-DRIVER'S LAMENT

My heart's on the footplate! I'm longing to be
In the cab of my dear old one-seventy-three*,
The hot oil, the coal smoke, the hissing of steam,
The crack of exhaust beats - alas, now a dream.
My heart's on the footplate! In fancy I feel
The throb of that mighty creation of steel
As she pounds up a grade - as she speeds o'er the plain
There is JOY in the rush of a swift moving train.
My heart's on the footplate! where'ere I may roam
The old Brighton line is to me 'Home Sweet Home';
But no longer its engines with echoing blast
And loud whistles, are there to recall days long past.
The 'milly-amp' trains no steam engines require,
Sparks fly blue from the 'juice rail' not red from a fire,
And though folk for electric or diesel may fall
A steam engine's cab is the best place of all.

December 1965   *Curly*
                                                   (LBSC)

*Note: LB & SCR No. 173 was Stroudley 0-4-2 *Cottesloe* of the Gladstone class.

Contents

AYESHA - the locomotive that began it all, sixty years ago.

FAYETTE - this superb example of one of LBSC's finest creations, now owned by George Barlow, was built by Tom Glazebrook who called her Victoria.

Foreword

FOREWORD by G. A. Barlow, B.E.M., Operarting Manager (retired) Romney Hythe & Dymchurch Railway

To a man who has spent most of his working life and a good deal of his spare time with small steam locomotives, it is an honour to be invited to write this foreword to Brian Hollingsworth's biography of 'Curly' Lawrence, a giant of universal renown in the world of miniature railway engines. I first read 'LBSC', as I knew him then, in the 1920s when I was at school, by borrowing the 'Model Engineer' from the Science Master and I have read this publication since those days - even through the period of the last war, when I was an engine driver on the standard gauge, serving with Royal Engineers - and I must have read just about every word that he wrote for 'the paper', as he always called it.

After over twenty years of reading and enjoying his brilliant writings, I finally met him in 1948, when he invited me to his home at Purley Oaks to drive 'Jeanie Deans', his 3½ins gauge Webb 3 Cylinder compound, which had so intrigued me when he described it in the 'Model Engineer' and we remained firm friends until his death in 1967. I ran most of his engines at Purley over the years and among my treasured possessions is a letter from 'Curly' in which he wrote, 'Come and have another run when you feel like it. I've plenty of engines!'

He visited the Barlow family on a number of occasions. A lover of children but denied them himself, our children helped him over his first visit to New Romney as with his shy and retiring nature, he had a terror of visiting strange places. I am sure that the presence of our son and daughter made a big difference to his visits when he was always accompanied by his wife, Mabel, a cheerful, friendly person.

Henry Greenly and others had shown the way with their excellent model locomotive work in the larger gauges but it was 'LBSC' who proved what could be done in the smaller sizes, so that coal burning, passenger hauling locomotives on 2½ins gauge became commonplace. They only became commonplace because of his real genius in describing how to build similar little machines to his own, so bringing their construction within the practical range of many people who would never have tackled such a job in other circumstances.

From this work has grown not only the vast number of small working steam locomotives in the world today but the development of Societies dedicated to the hobby and to the building of splendid, continuous passenger carrying tracks many of which are in existence, I feel sure, solely due to the influence of 'LBSC'. So numerous have such tracks become that it is now possible to visit several in this country in the course of a single day and the pleasure that is thus given to an enormous number of people is immeasurable; a truly wonderful memorial to a great man.

Because of 'Curly's' unusual make-up and his reclusive style of life for many years, writing his biography calls for a man not only with literary talent but also possessing gentleness and sensitivity in his nature. An engineer by profession and a passionate lover of the steam locomotive in all its sizes, Brian Hollingsworth, author of a number of books on railway matters, is just the man to execute what could not have been an easy task but it is a book that *had* to be written to remind us all, young and not so young, of 'Curly's' enormous achievements.

George Barlow

Lillian 'Curly' Lawrence, better known in his later years as 'L.B.S.C.' of the Model Engineer, was throughout his life an enigmatic and rather private person; never is this better illustrated than when one investigates the date and circumstances of his birth. If one makes deductions from hints dropped from time to time in his writings, one finds such remarks as 'I joined the railway in 1894 just before my 16th birthday'. He did actually go so far as to tell one friend that he was born in 1878, while another got a hint when he said as a train went by his house 'that locomotive's number is the year I was born'. The friend failed to see the number but the old Southern Railway did have a gap in their number series from 1881 to 1889. Another friend was told that the birth year was the same as Winston Churchill's; yet Winston was born in 1874! But other references point to a birth-year of 1882 or 1883.

It is true also that the ages given on both his death and his marriage certificates point to a birthday in 1882 and 1883. And over all the years in question the only Lillian Lawrence whose birth was registered in England and Wales was described as the daughter of William Lawrence, Coachman, and his wife Elizabeth on 12th December 1882 at 12 Devonport Mews, Paddington, London. I think it should be accepted that this child was Curly; it is even today quite common for male newly-born babies to be mistaken for female. What is peculiar is that his registration entry was never altered to suit, as is normally done in such cases; in which case the secret would remain hidden in the Registrar-General's archives.

The first home that Curly remembered was on the first floor of an apartment house in Peckham, but long before he went to school they moved to a small house, No. 25, The Crescent, Peckham (now known as Clifton Crescent), just off Meeting House Lane. The nickname reflected his possession of a fine head of long golden curls; as was quite often the custom for small boys in those days, his mother dressed him as a girl. Although her son was blond he in fact had long dark hair and his rather unsatisfactory father was also dark-haired. Curly's existence was barely acknowledged by this man who was often away for weeks at a time. 'I don't know to this day what he did' wrote Curly in later years.

Curly's own marriage certificate of 1908 is more specific; this describes the father's occupation as "Chemist" but it was a shock to find the name given as Henry Mathieson. Other references to this man describe him as Henry Morris Mathieson, Master Lithographer, and Morris Mathieson, Dentist, so no wonder our young hero got a little confused. However, several cross-bearing in the way of letters and diaries intersect to indicate that, in spite of what his birth certificate tells us. C. was the child of this person and a lady called Eleanor Mathieson, née Everett.

The only plausible explanation for these apparently contradictory facts would seem to be that Curly arrived before the couple had decided to marry. When her time was due Eleanor was sent way across London to these reliable Lawrences - possibly friends of the family - to have the baby. In order to avoid the stigma of illegitimacy the child was registered as the Lawrences' own, although Eleanor took it back with her to Peckham.

Later, as we know, little Lillian turned out to be a boy but then, having once played ducks and drakes with the system Eleanor was

Curly's mother - almost certainly.

reluctant to draw attention to the circumstance of its registration by asking for the gender entry to be changed; otherwise it is difficult to explain why someone as sensible as Curly's mama evidently was did not have this done. So Curly was saddled with a female birth certificate - which must have been an embarrassment to him as a young man. Later as we shall see, he came not only to accept but also to welcome it.

Soon enough, though (although the date is not known) his parents got married and had further children. A boy called Rudolph Benjamin - Curly referred to him as "Rue" in his diaries - was born in 1894 and there is reference in the live Steam notes to a sister who emigrated to Canada and lived in Toronto.

Eleanor Mathieson died in 1942 at 80 Asylum Road, Peckham, aged 85, but Henry (so Curly told George Murray of Manchester, Connecticut in a letter) continued wandering and died in Scotland while still quite young. While he was alive he contributed little to the family budget and his wife had to work long hours with her needle in an attempt to keep the family together. There was also more than a hint that a drink problem existed; Curly compensated for his father's weakness in this respect by never touching alcohol as long as he lived.

In spite of the family being poor, Curly remembered his childhood as a very happy one. He was healthy, bright, strong and well loved at home; his principal pleasure - that of watching the trains go by - was free of charge. In 1950 he wrote as follows............

Maybe, as I roll on toward the terminal station of the great Railroad of Life, I'm getting a bit pernickety, in a manner of speaking; but the above-mentioned 'Merry Christmas and Happy New Year' seems to sound rather hollow nowadays; when I was a child, the meaning seemed literal. The first Christmas of which I have distinct recollection, was in the early eighties of the last century, when I was but four years of age. Mother and granny went out on the Christmas eve to do a little shopping; not much as we were very poor. I went with them, and I remember how gay the High Street looked, with all the shops decorated up, and well stocked with good things. There were crowds of people, too, and all were cheerful and smiling. Many of the street tramway cars, small four-wheeled vehicles, were drawn by three mules running abreast; and one old red-faced white-bearded driver, who bore a striking resemblance to the legendary Santa Claus, decorated up the mules' harness with sprigs of holly and mistletoe, tied a small bell to each of their collars, and put on a red hat. There was great delight and much 'hooraying' from the kiddies as the tramway-car rattled along the High

AJAX - price 6s. 6d, Curly's first locomotive.

Street, to the clattering of the mules' hooves and the jingling of the bells; in the kiddies' estimation, it was the next best thing to seeing the real Santa and his reindeer-hauled sleigh. The day was frosty, though the sun was bright and there was a keen wind. I was wearing a wool coat and a wool tam-o'-shanter which I had pulled down over my ears, to prevent them being 'nipped'; and granny bought me a pair of woollen gloves for a Christmas box, to save me from chilblains on my fingers. Mother bought me a big bag of sweets for a penny, and I was supremely happy, without a care in the wide world.

In later years he often recalled with nostalgic longing a ballad his mother used to sing to him.......

'Backward, flow backward
O time in your flight -
Make me a child again
Just for tonight'

In one way in particular, all we Live Steamers owe a great debt of gratitude to Curly's capable and lovely mum; because, in spite of such extreme poverty that they barely had enough to eat, she saw to it that Curly was properly educated, first at a small private school, then at a larger but still independent one. From all accounts this second school was very good. Certainly Curly received an excellent education as his stupendous literary achievements testify.

He tells of having reached the top class at the age of eleven. Any problems with his fellow schoolboys on the grounds of sissiness were precluded because 'Dolly' (as he was known at school) had physical strength well above average. Although having a natural talent for them, he didn't enjoy organised games but described one occasion when, having reluctantly turned out for a school cricket match (at Southwark Park - the match was against Ilderton Road Schools) he hit sixes all over the place. All this to the amazement and chagrin of the opposition, who found themselves losing the match on account of this 'girl' with the long golden locks. They had been tactfully hidden under the tam o'shanter hat - until someone pulled it off.

His mother's mother lived with them. She was over 50 when Curly was born and eight years a widow. Granny was supported by her son, who lived nearby and working in a City eating-house, where Curly could always rely on getting a meal when he was old enough to move around on his own. Granny gave Curly her husband's tools, which included a soldering bit. This the boy soon learned to use and was able to earn a few much-need coppers repairing the neighbour's pots and pans. He also built his first steam locomotive, based on the Borough's steam roller, with a soldered up coffee tin for the boiler and press-in type lids for wheels. A broken toy steam engine was the basis of the mechanism, which was mounted on top of the boiler, driving one of the lids by a cotton belt, as shewn below.

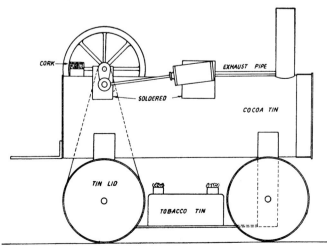

Curly's Mama allowed him considerable freedom from an early age to go off on his own. Her only proviso was that he should say when he was going to be back and always keep to it. This he always did and thus won her confidence. So, with the aid of the money earned by doing repairs to pots and pans Curly was enabled to indulge his passion for seeing railways and locomotives; not only the ochre one of his native Peckham but the green (several shades), black, blue and red ones of other parts of London also. There were trips on the steam underground and Curly was an early customer on the first tube in December 1891, a few months after it opened. The terminus at Stockwell was within walking distance of his home.

The City and South London tube trains had air brakes worked from a reservoir which could be replenished from a compressed air supply available at either terminus. Seeing a small girl wistfully looking up at the cab, the driver asked her in. His expression when 'missy' (a voracious reader at the local library) asked some searching technical questions would - as Curly wrote fifty years later - have made his fortune in Hollywood. On these early expeditions to London, Curly pressed his small nose against shop windows behind which such delights ass early brass steam railway locomotives were displayed for sale. Alas, for him an Ajax at over five shillings was as far out of reach as a full-size Stroudley single; but he reckoned without Granny who one day offered him this sum to buy one. He was able to make up the difference himself.

However, like the man who was told (in respect of a steam yacht) that if he had to ask the price he couldn't afford it, Curly found the running cost on methylated spirits a bit fierce. Which turned his mind to a solid fuel such as charcoal; this a friendly florist would supply him *gratis* being grateful for services rendered. A firebox - literally so - was fitted and worked well; it was also unaffected by the breeze, which blew the spirit flames away from the boiler. Alas, Ajax's tin boiler rusted away and so had a short life, but the remainder formed the basis of a second and far superior edition. This had a brass frame, copper boiler, and various other refinements. Even so, it was a long way from a proper locomotive.

But in the meantime there had been a happening that was a milestone in Curly's life. One day he was taking the short cut home from school via his local station, Queen's Road, when he passed the station master who was talking to one of the drivers from the local New Cross Dept. A gust of wind swept away some papers which were being discussed between the two of them; these Curly rescued. Introductions followed, the station master explaining that this was the little boy who ran his own small steam engine, whereupon the driver asked him if he would like to drive a big one!

An assignation was made for twelve-year old Curly to be on the platform that very evening. The train concerned was the 5.52 from Peckham Rye to Shoreditch. The route lay through Brunel's Tunnel under the Thames at Rotherhithe, known then like now as the East London line. The London, Brighton & South Coast Railway ran it with their famous 0-6-0T 'Terrier' Tank locomotives and set trains of four-wheel carriages. Today the service is operated by London Transport tube trains and runs from New Cross or New Cross Gate rather than Peckham Rye. Anyway, Curly was waiting on the platform when No. 55 *Stepney*, clean as a new pin, ran in with seven four-wheelers. He had a certain 'stage fright' at first but once they had passed under the river all nervousness had gone.

In Curly's own words............

From there to the end of the journey, I just watched, and asked questions. The fireman had only fired once; how long did the engine run and how far did she go on one firing? The water in the gauge glass was keeping level; how was the pump regulated? I learned that she had two pumps, not only one as on the steam roller, and one was pumping all the time, the other as needed. I told the driver that I could drive a steam roller, and understood about that pretty well; so he said the railway engine was pretty much the same, only it went a little faster (I'll say it did!) and did not have to be steered. He explained about the cylinder lubricator and the air brake, and several other things, being agreeably surprised to find I had some sort of 'foundation knowledge' and could quickly pick up details.

When we stopped at the terminal (Shoreditch) he stepped aside and said 'See if you're strong enough to pull the lever back, Curly', so poor Curly took his courage - and the lever! - in both hands, gave a mighty tug and over it came. 'Good', said the driver. 'Well, you're going to do the shunting'. At that I nearly had another fainting fit, but bit my lips and said rather shakily, 'Please tell me what to do, and I'll try'. When the passengers had all gone, the shunting signal at the end of the platform changed to green and the driver said, 'Now, Curly, give her a little steam', so for the first time in my life, I took hold of the regulator handle of the real railway engine, moved it, and felt the engine move backwards very gently, pushing the empty train before it. At that instant an indefinable 'something' seemed to enter my very being, which has remained with me all through the years, and which has caused many folk to refer to me as 'a steam locomotive in human form'; it is a kind of affinity I can't explain. It is the one thing I shall never forget; a sort of 'permanent electric shock' if you get my meaning. Anyway suffice it to say that the driver told me when and where to shut off and apply the brake. The fireman uncoupled her; I reversed her, ran light to the crossover, went back on the other road, crossed over again, and with the driver ready at the handle of the handbrake in case I made a slip, actually managed to run her up to the carriages and 'touch buffers'. To make certain of it, I stopped her dead about a carriage length from the train, then eased up and the fireman gave me the sign when the buffers were about a foot apart. I then pushed the train back to the other platform, the driver telling me where to apply the brake to stop in the proper place; and then the driver took charge once more.

The return journey was made, of course, with the little engine running bunker first, and as it was now dark, there was no difference between running in the tunnels and in the open air section from Deptford Road (now called Surrey Docks) to Peckham Rye. The driver showed me the difference between chimney-first and bunker-first operation, and when we arrived at Peckham Rye and pulled into the siding where the electric depot now stands he made me do the shunt again. At this end, the train ran from the siding into the station with the engine leading; and the driver said as I had made the shunt, I had better finish the job and take her in, but be sure and stop with the middle part of the train opposite the ticket barrier. I managed it; and then he said, 'Now, Curly, be plucky and drive yourself home'. The green light on the up local starting signal seemed to wink encouragement; and so it came

to pass that when the guard's green lamp waved from down the platform it was Curly's somewhat grubby fist that gave the response on 'Stepney's' whistle, and very gingerly opened the regulator. As the little engine responded, and puffed heartily across the bridge spanning brightly-lighted Rye Lane, there wasn't a prouder or happier kid in the whole wide world. As we passed the coal yard on the left, I managed to get the lever back next notch to middle; but migosh! *Didn't* it want some shifting against the pull of the eccentrics. It was only a couple of minutes run to my home station, and by shutting off steam at the second bridge - not forgetting first to open the blower and put the lever in full gear after, and then making the brake application just before reaching the signal box, the little engine pulled up exactly at the place where I had boarded her some two hours or so before, in fear and trepidation. And when the ticket collector waved me through the barrier with a smiling 'Goodnight driver!' my cup of happiness just overflowed. Michael Rynold's oft-repeated assertion that 'a child can drive a Stroudley engine' was that night proved absolutely correct.

So Curly in a kind of way followed in this great grandfather's footsteps - he drove a stage coach from Marble Arch to Stanmore before the railways came - and settled what was to be the great driving force in his life. In the days to come Curly enjoyed many more engine-driving trips on *Stepney* and, indeed, other excursions because the driver and his wife - a jolly but childless couple - befriended him and took him around on their days off. The driver, in fact, became the father Curly never had.

In the meantime, there was a problem - school the next morning. Star-pupil Dolly, instead of applying himself to his lessons, had his mind on other things and it was noticed; but the old schoolmaster was one of those who didn't do things by the book. Having found the cause, young Lawrence's 'punishment', believe it or not, was an extra-mural essay on the steam locomotive.

So the first live-steam note came to be written, telling the story from the moment when Billy Murdock scared the parson out of his wits that night in the churchyard at Camborne; right up to the last word in steam express locomotives - the Stirling eight foot singles on the Great Northern and Stroudley's 2-2-2s on the Brighton line. After he had read it the teacher sent it up to the headmaster, who praised the essay and gave Curly a shilling (a princely sum for a child in those days) as a reward. In writing of this incident late in 1941, Curly wrote of it occurring 'just over fifty years ago'. This again indicated a birth year before 1880, but he tended to be casual about dates, as we have seen.

This teacher, incidentally, used to keep his class absolutely enthralled; he was a much-travelled man and would not teach 'from the book' as was and is usual in the school teaching profession. Instead he would tell what he had seen and done when he actually went to the places mentioned in the lesson. So when it came to Curly's turn to teach, he followed this example, as we shall see.

In the meantime, Curly longed to build himself a better locomotive and, like many similar aspirants since, the problem was the necessity for a machine tool of some kind and hence funds to buy it. One day he was walking back from a train-spotting expedition to London and in the window of an ironmongery shop near the Elephant and Castle he saw a lathe. It was about 2½in. centres and 2ft. long and complete with stand and treadle. The cost was 30 shillings. The storekeeper (also a steam enthusiast) was amazed but sympathetic when Curly told him shyly what he wanted it for.

Anyway, he was offered the lathe for a pound; not only that, it would be kept for him for six weeks on payment of a shilling deposit.

To appreciate the nature of the task ahead one might imagine a boy from an unemployed family of the present day trying to earn £100 or so needed to buy a simple lathe today, by doing chores for the neighbours. To cut a long story short, he did it just within the time limit by dint of a heavy sales campaign for his usual services, plus some unusual ones like acting as a model for a dressmaker and reading to a newspaper reporter so that he could practice his shorthand. When the lathe was brought home, there was, as Curly found out only too easily, the problem that for it to be of any use, nearly as much needed to be spent on accessories as on the original lathe. Even so, he persevered with what bits and pieces he could scrounge, aided by information obtained from books borrowed from the library.

Nevertheless, he (now aged 13 or so) built a steam locomotive which really did bear some resemblance to a full-size one. This was after he had acquired a broken relic similar to *Ajax*, from a junk shop for threepence. With parts salvaged from both Ajax locomotives he built what was something like a Stroudly 'D' class 0-4-2T. It not only puffed, but also could be reversed by a lever in the cab, using a fourway cock. His driver friend took nearly as much interest in it as Curly did himself. Later there was a track - with rails made from old umbrella ribs - for it to run on.

But by now the time was approaching when young Lawrence was to start his apprenticeship to the steam locomotive for real, as a cleaner boy at New Cross Dept. This he did before his 16th birthday, losing his golden mop in the process. 'Short back and sides' was very much the rule then in railway service.

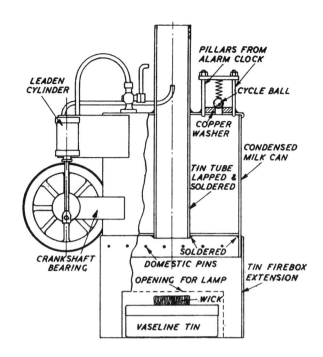

When Curly acquired his lathe, the first model he built was this stationary steam engine.

When Ajax' boiler rusted through, some of its parts were incorporated in what was something-like-a-Stroudley 'D' class 0-4-2T with two oscillating cylinders.

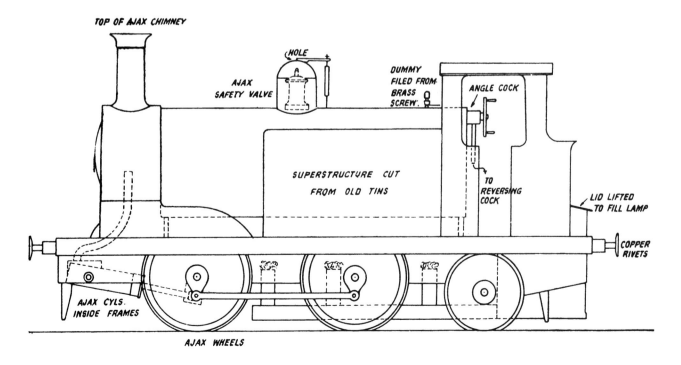

The New Cross Locomotive Depot of the London, Brighton and South Coast Railway was a mere ten minutes walk from home when Curly (now less curly than he used to be) achieved his dearest ambition of working there. However, the years he spent on the footplate remain, like his birth, rather a mystery. Amongst the several million words he wrote on locomotives, packed with autobiographical material, virtually no L. B. & S. C. R. locomotive experiences are described directly. There are plenty of impersonal descriptions of cleaning, firing and driving locomotives on the old Brighton line and also of life in the sheds; yet personal reminiscence and example was the whole basis of Curly's style, as well as the secret of its success. Moreover, locomotive working was the very heart of what he wrote about. This omission is certainly significant.

Even so, we do see him at his interview being asked questions on signals by the shed foreman who dryly remarked 'seen these once or twice before, haven't you Curly?'. His antics on *Stepney* had not gone un-noticed by higher authority! Then there comes a click and a shutter drops and we hear that cleaners got 2 shillings (10p) per day (firemen 5 shillings, drivers 8 shillings) and worked a ten-hour day or shift exclusive of meal breaks. He describes how the work was organised and the actual process of cleaning locomotives by the use of elbow grease mainly, aided by cotton waste oil, tallow and in bad cases powdered bath-brick, soft soap and emery cloth. The copper caps of the chimneys were given a final bobbing with soot from inside the chimney. Of course, in present day terms one would not call it cleaning; just a process of making already-too-clean locomotives even cleaner. As Curly wrote 'only let a fussy driver find any tiny fillet of dirt left in the joint between wheel and tyre, such as the local window cleaner today (it was 1940) leaves round every pane and see what happened - probably "on the carpet" for the culprit!, but on the whole the cleaners took a pride in their work, vying with one another for the shiniest results!

When first started a boy worked in a gang of six or so lads under an experienced man from 6.00 a.m. to 5.30 p.m., with a 45 minute break for breakfast and 60 minutes for lunch. When he knew the job he was given an engine to 'follow' and thereafter he worked when that locomotive was 'on shed'. New boys were ragged a bit, but if they took no offence and gave as good as they got they would become accepted. Even so, I dare say Curly never fell for that one about fetching red oil from the stores for filling he tail lamp. Anyway, there were lots of pranks and good-natured fun; New Cross was (by Curly's account, anyway) a friendly place. Exceptionally, Curly described an occasion when he was amongst a group of lads who found a locomotive with the valve-chest covers off; they used a pinch bar to move the engine and see how the slide valves were set. The shed foreman caught them at it , but in the end settled for them to listen to a dissertation on valve-setting as a punishment. Also exceptionally, he wrote very late in life about his first Christmas in the sheds, when he volunteered for solitary duty rather than stay in his slightly cheerless home.

In due time (the norm was about four years then) he passed the various tests as a fireman and went out on the road. For a young fireman, rides on other companies' locomotives were a possibility;

a cap, sooty engineman's clothes a union badge were as good as a country-wide footplate pass. Curly describes (in November 1937) a hell-for-leather ride from Rugby to Willesden Junction on a heavily thrashed 'Jumbo' 2-4-0, the 77½ miles being run in 82 minutes. *The Auditor* had a mixed train of bogies and six wheelers, 48 axles in all. He writes.....

> 'then we came to the long bank up to Tring. It was now dark and the old *Auditor* going all out was a sight I shall ever remember - the top of the chimney looked like what I should imagine Mount Vesuvius looked like in the last days of Pompeii; red, orange and blue flames and millions of sparks and red-hot lumps; honestly , I believe a Brighton 'Terrier' could have run on what she threw away. The firehole was just like an electric arc lamp; how the firebars stayed put instead of melting up was a marvel, but the old cat absolutely seemed to enjoy it, she blew off steadily the whole time even with both injectors on!'

As he proceeded home from Willesden via Addison Road and Clapham Junction, Curly wondered what would happen to a fragile Brighton 'Billington' 4-4-0 if a typical North-Western crew had it on a tight schedule!

Another 'Old Slide in the Magic Lantern' (his phrase) described how in 1902 he decided to buy one of the legendary Drummond 3½in. lathes (these magnificent tools were still in production 45 years later when the writer bought his) then advertised at £13.10s. He travelled in uniform to Guildford - L. B. & S. C. R. employees went free when so clad - and saw Mr. Arthur Drummond himself, who let him have it on easy terms commensurate with his 30 shillings a week pay as a fireman.

The extra money also went into a better model railway. He was able to obtain a quantity of loose tin rails from Archbutts, an optician's shop in Westminster Bridge Road. Builders' laths were used to make sleepers, the combination making a first class permanent way.

In addition to his 'D' class tank, rebuilt from *Ajax* bits, he now had a single-wheeler of a design based on a cast bedplate and of which the parts were made by a firm called Sutclifffe, as well as other locomotives. Of course, the Model Engineer was now appearing - Curly took it from No. 1 - and this was a great help to someone who until now had been feeling his way in the dark.

There is a reason to suppose that the gauge of this first proper Curly Railway was 2¹¹⁄₁₆ in. and as his people had apparently now moved to a house with a garden, the line could be a permanent one. It became quite elaborate and had a remote control system connected with the signals; movable ramps beside the line stopped and started the trains as well as blew the whistle. Curly writes....

> 'It was a peculiar experience to leave the distant and home signals at danger and see the baby locomotive cease puffing, whistle the distant and slow down as it approached the home; then if you suddenly pulled off the home it would give the regulation toot and puff up to speed again in the manner usually observed by its full-sized sisters.'

In 1899 the L. B. & S. C. R. had a collision in fog at Bermondsey between London Bridge and New Cross. Young Lawrence put proposals forward for a cab signalling system, but he was only able to install it on his own model line.

It is possible that the locomotives which ran on this line were

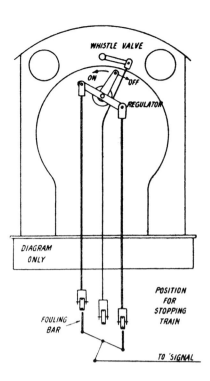

How the signals controlled the trains.

those described in the Model Engineer for 24th September and 8th October, 1903, in a two-part article entitled "Four Simple Locomotives". The article is not signed but the author is the same person who wrote a short letter which appeared in the 1st August 1902 issue, signed "J. M. W., Peckham". The style is similar to Curly's and, whilst no connection can be proved - apart from residence in Peckham - I think it is likely that this was Curly's debut as a technical journalist. Remember that in those days railway employees were totally forbidden to make any contribution to the press, however innocent, on pain of dismissal; hence the alias.

The four locomotives (0-6-0 *Stoke Bassett*, 4-4-0 *Zulu*, 0-4-4T *Ferndale* and 2-4-2 *Ecclesbourne*) were built to $2\frac{11}{16}$in. gauge and were indeed very simple. Their pot boilers were fired with spirit and they all used oscillating cylinders and those with two cylinders had single-acting ones; the exception was *Ferndale* which had one double-acting inside oscillating cylinder. *Ferndale* was also tried with a simple homemade paraffin vaporising burner, also described. Although so elementary as regards their "works", all four locos had such details as working spring buffers, proper couplings and removable headlights. They also looked like proper locomotives and in all these ways might well have been originally Curly creations. A point is that none of them would have been self-starting and this fits nicely with the description of the control

system above which implies that you had to pull off the home signal while the train was still in motion. For someone equipped with a proper lathe, there would have been no problems in making up the locomotives in a few weeks even though, in typical Curly style, almost every part was built from scratch. A comment in the article that the locomotives were built using a small 17s. 6d. lathe was corrected in a following "Smoke Ring" which mentioned a 3in. lathe.

Locomotives such as these described (even if these actual ones were not Curly's) with oscillating cylinders were very much of the toy kind, but with the Drummond lathe in the workshop and the Model Engineer on his bookshelf Curly was able at last to have a go at building a proper locomotive. The chosen prototype was L. B. & S. C. R. Stroudley 'Jumbo' goods 0-6-0 No. 430 and the design was based on one published by Henry Greenly in the Model Engineer. It went well but its builder felt it could do better; amongst other things, he queried the then accepted doctrine that expansion of steam was not possible in small cylinders because of condensation.

One day he decided to alter the valve gear and valve so that the valve events corresponded as closely as possible to a full-size 'Jumbo' (he went and checked on one in the shed) allowing for the fact that his ⅛th full-size model had only a single cylinder and slip-eccentric valve gear. He did all this and discovered that an immense improvement resulted; from then on in his locomotive work he never again accepted the printed word as gospel. It was a turning point in his career.

But it must be clear that a more basic 'divine discontent' had made Curly dissatisfied with his work. Of course, as a locomotive fireman he was, as it were, a racehorse between the shafts of a milk-float. Electric trams and early motor buses were competing hard for the L. B. & S. C. R.'s traffic and so promotion was slow. But one part of the railway system was expanding, to wit, the London Underground; drivers' jobs were going and men with experience on steam railways would have an advantage. So Curly became for a time a driver of early 'Milly-Amp' (electric) trains beneath London streets; but his until now always excellent health suffered from life below ground and he was soon advised by his doctor to take an open air job. Incidentally, it must be said that in later years he sometimes 'swung the lead' just a little in his writing, not actually saying but still implying that he had had considerable experience as a *steam* driver on the old 'L. B. & S. C. R. '. Later also he described this move (with only partial accuracy, I think) as 'a search for a bigger pay-packet - the greatest mistake I ever made in my life!'. Of course, we more normal mortals envy genius but those who have it often regard their state and what it drives them to do as a burden to be borne rather than a talent to be enjoyed. I think Curly felt this way for long periods during his life.

This contemporary picture of the LB&SCR 2-2-2 Grosvenor shows the standard of cleanliness during Curly's time on the railway. The original postcard was sent by Curly to Geoffrey Cashmore. The reverse side is shown on page 101.

After Curly had left the electric railway, he stayed on the rails and became a tram driver. The photograph shows him (presumably on his passing-out day) at the controls of LCC Tramways class 'C' car No. 255 at Rye Lane Depot, Peckham. The date is known fairly accurately because this particular car was delivered in 1903 and in 1905 was fitted with a covered top.

A few years later he finally forsook the rails to drive motor buses. He worked for the British Electric Traction Company which then had (in spite of the name) a number of *motor* bus routes in London and a fleet of buses with the name BRITISH on the sides.

Of course he continued to build models but being now well on in his twenties like most men he could not ignore what he once described very charmingly......

> ... and just about this time Dame Nature asserted herself. A feminine voice was quietly but persistently calling - through the sound of whistles, safety valves blowing off, chonk of exhaust beats, and rattle and clatter of trains, both large and small - and I knew the time had come when I must make a home of my own. So I dismantled the bits and pieces (of my railway) scrapped what was useless, laid aside the rest for future use, and devoted myself to other matters for the time being; and it came to pass that one bright January morning I steamed proudly out of Church Junction on the Great Railroad of Life with not so much coal and water in the tender, but a darn good mate in the shape of a little soft-voiced dark-haired Scottish lassie not yet out of her teens. That was over a quarter of a century ago; we are still plodding steadily along and haven't had to burn the footboards yet to keep steam in the boiler, though once or twice we've been perilously near it. Also we have seen lots of orange lights, and occasionally a red one, but it has always turned green in the nick of time - Fate, though unkind, sometimes has what the radio announcer calls 'bright intervals'!

The marriage took place at St. Phillips Church, Camberwell on 2nd January 1908, in fact not quite half a century before he wrote the above in the Model Engineer for 11th May 1932. Curly gave his name as Lillian Lawrence, 24, Motor Driver of 243 Queen's Road, Peckham. He married Mabel Munt, 19, daughter of Thomas

Tram-driver Lawrence at Rye Lane Depot, Peckham.

Munt, Labourer, of 1, German Street, Camberwell. One might comment that it is odd that Curly should have used his feminine 'given' name on the one occasion above all others that a young man needs to be thought particularly masculine.

The young couple found a small self-contained flat in Dulwich. The bill for furnishing it has survived, the earliest documents known which for certain concerns our hero....

<table>
<tr><td colspan="4">Bought of C. DOWNING & SONS</td></tr>
<tr><td colspan="4">49, 50 & 51 London Road, SOUTHWARK, S.E.</td></tr>
<tr><td colspan="4">Near The Elephant and Castle</td></tr>
<tr><td>Compete House Furnishers</td><td colspan="3">19/12/07</td></tr>
<tr><td>Suite</td><td>£5.</td><td>12.</td><td>6</td></tr>
<tr><td>Wardrobe, Dr. Chest, Washstand</td><td>£5.</td><td>17.</td><td>6</td></tr>
<tr><td>2 Cane chairs</td><td></td><td>6.</td><td>0</td></tr>
<tr><td>4ft. bedstead, Wire Matt., Matt.</td><td>£11.</td><td>16.</td><td>0</td></tr>
<tr><td>2 Pillows</td><td>£3.</td><td>0.</td><td>0</td></tr>
<tr><td>K. Table, 8/6, 3 Chairs, 10/6,</td><td></td><td></td><td></td></tr>
<tr><td>K. Fender 3/6, Irons 3/0</td><td>£1.</td><td>5.</td><td>6</td></tr>
<tr><td>Coal Box 6/6, Table 18/6</td><td>£1.</td><td>5.</td><td>-</td></tr>
<tr><td>Cabinet</td><td>£2.</td><td>9.</td><td>6</td></tr>
<tr><td></td><td>£19.</td><td>16.</td><td>0</td></tr>
</table>

As many model rail nuts have found since, model railways and new wives are not always possible in combination. The Lawrences new abode has no garden; so no possibility of continuing to have and run an elaborate scenic line existed. Curly made a big step forward when in 1910 he took a job involving testing and

Lillian Lawrence during his bus-driving days.

Mabel Lawrence.

experimental work for the Daimler Motor Car Company. Rather than move from south London where he and Mabel had their relations he travelled daily the 90 miles to Coventry by rail, making the journey six times a week with a season ticket whose cost worked out at seven miles for an (old) penny!

Bradshaw for April 1910 gives the following possibilities for his daily schedule.......

	a.m.	a.m.		p.m.
Euston	5.00	7.10	Coventry	6.00
Rugby	6.48	8.59	Rugby	6.19
(change)	7.05	9.10	(change)	6.33
Coventry	7.29	9.29	Euston	8.10

To this must be added the local journey of six miles between Dulwich and Euston; local train services would be small help in catching the first mentioned train. I don't know about the trams but a bicycle would certainly be a possibility.

Some might consider this commuting epic too tedious for words, but remember that Curly was as avid a rail fan as ever walked this earth. Moreover - and this is very difficult fo us to realise - railways in Britain were at their Zenith and the saying 'British and Best' was no figure of speech, just a plain statement of the way things were. And of the great railways of Britain the London and North Western Railway was known with reason as the Premier Line. All this meant standards of reliability, punctuality, cleanliness and service which we today find impossible to believe could ever exist.

Curly had some wonderful runs behind the 'blackberry black' motive power of the London & North Western Railway; on his regular train, the 6.33 p.m. from Rugby, 'George-the-Fifth' 4-4-0 *Cedric* once brought 11 coaches up to London in 77½ minutes for the 82½ miles. On another occasion he travelled up from Birmingham behind a '19-inch goods' 4-6-0 - with only 5 ft. 2in. driving wheels - which kept the two-hour schedule for the 123 miles. There can have been little time in his life for model locomotive work - but this was made up for by these big helpings of full-size trains.

Even so, in the February 1912 issue of the now sadly defunct journal *Models, Railways and Locomotives*, editor Henry Greenly wrote......

'Our anonymous contributor of the excellent article on the making of a small steam locomotive has been know to us as an enthusiastic amateur of the 'make-as-much-as-you-can-yourself' school for some years. He built model locomotives from the simplest materials and with the simplest tools in the early days of the present era successful working models. His experiences are, therefore, worthy of every consideration by those whose model-making career is not so extensive'.

This referred to an article "The Development of a Successful Smale Scale Locomotive" and the pen-name of the writer was set down as "Lylia". In the very first paragraph a reference to "brother locomotive superintendents of the 2in. gauge" is such an absolutely typical 'LBSC' remark that in conjunction with the similarity of the pseudonym to Curly's first name there can be little doubt of the identity of the author.

The story tells how a little short-wheelbase 0-6-0 tank locomotive was developed over a period of years. In 1904 when the engine was built, it had a vertical geared engine with one single-acting oscillating cylinder and a "pot" boiler, spirit-fired whose only claim to sophistication lay in having three water types underneath. Later, the engine was fitted with an horizontally arranged cylinder, driving through spur gears until finally replaced by a double-acting oscillating cylinder driving the leading axle direct.

Most interesting and significant was the simple superheated locomotive-type boiler which was the next improvement. This had a single oval fire-tube or flue fitted with five ½ inch diameter cross water-tubes. There was alternative firing using either a two-wick spirit lamp ("for ordinary use") and a small vapourising petrol burner 'for heavy work'. The results were excellent and no doubt Curly's later predilection for the relatively complex locomotive-type boiler stemmed from this. He adds that the locomotive was finished in the "dark umber of the LB&SCR, lined yellow and black, with the name in green shaded letters on the tanks". Alas, he never said what the name was and the lettering has not come out in the illustration; accordingly, this locomotive is catalogued under the name *Lylia*.

His next job was promotion in the world as he became a travelling inspector for Messrs. Thomas Tilling, a well-known transport firm based in London, which ran a combined fleet of buses and lorries. The only thing we know about this job is a description of an incident when Curly was out with the Big Boss in one of the firm's cars - which then did not come within Curly's orbit - and the state of its steering convinced the Chief that they should do so in the future. In consequence, he and Mabel were able to move into a rented house on the Old Brighton Road (now called London Road) just south of Norbury Station on the Victoria to Brighton main line. With a little more leisure and a little more money at his disposal, Curly was able to undertake a little engineering on his own behalf. He equipped his house with an electric light plant, driven by a ¾h.p. oil engine and set up his workshop on the 'first floor back'. In addition to making little locomotives, he was considering a steam version of one of the rather rickety so-called cycle cars then on the market. But then, as he said, a certain party who wore a spike on his hat threw a spanner in the works.

When the Kaiser's war came in 1914, Curly found himself in an excepted occupation and, moreover, right on the military age limit. Even so, he got swept up by the great munition drive of 1916-17 and he was put in charge of a small factory set up in Weybridge, Surrey, to produce aero engine parts. It was 18 miles from Norbury and one would have thought a miniscule commuting effort compared with what had gone before, but the Ministry of

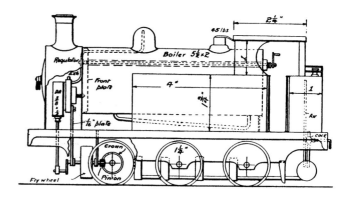

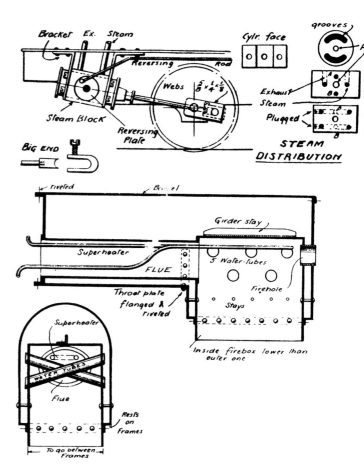

LYLIA's 0-6-0T locomotive in its first and in its final stages of development.

Munitions advised him to buy a Model T Ford car and allowed him petrol for it.

He had 37 girls put under him; on Day One he assembled his little army and explained the way things were going to be. That we know such detail as nearly all their names is something new in this account of Curly's career; and since we do so because he wrote verse to them, you may realise that factory life under Manager Lawrence was far from conventional. Hardly great poetry, but great fun were...

There was a young lady named Kate
Five mornings a week she was late;
She said 'If I fix
The alarm clock for six
It usually rings about eight!'

There was a young lady named Ida
She didn't care what might betide her;
But the yell that she gave
Proved she wasn't so brave
When she found a black beetle beside her.

There was a young lady named Letty
Whose hair was exceedingly pretty
Till she had it cut short
and the hat that she bought
Looked as though it was trimmed with confetti.

There was a young lady named Brenda
Always hurried wherever you'd send her
But one day sad to tell
Near the stove, down she fell
And she got a black eye on the fender.

There was a young lady named Hilda
The big capstan lathe simply thrilled her;
She worked it with skill
Though she looked frail and ill,
You'd have thought such a job would have killed her.

There was a young lady named Pat
Came to work in a lovely new hat
But the breeze from the door
Blew it right up the floor
And a belt caught and squashed it quite flat!

There was a young lady named Kitty
Goodlooking and cheerful and witty;
She was fond of a smoke
And could crack a good joke -
She had learned quite a lot in the City!

There was a young lady named Nellie
Loved Blancmanges, and ice-cream and jelly;
She thought it no feat
Fifteen ices to eat
So she must have a cast iron bel - sorry, tummy.

There was a young lady named Milly
When a tool broke cried 'mend it, please, Billy
Or you'll take all the onus
For stopping my bonus
And making me look such a silly.'

There was a young lady named Joyce
She had a most musical voice
In a search near and far
For an opera star
She'd have certainly been the first choice.

There was a young lady named Mary
In her work she was ever so wary;
All the pins that she ground
Were dead size and all round -
Not a single hair's breadth would they vary.

There was a young lady named Winnie
Met her bashful boyfriend in the spinney;
He stammered 'Please miss
Would you spare me a kiss?'
'Fancy asking!' she laughed, 'Oh, the ninny'.

There was a young lady named Jewel
Her chuck knocked the tip off the tewel;
She said 'What a mutt
For not stopping the cut -
Oh, I feel such an absolute fewel!'

There was a young lady named Ann
Every day a fresh job she began;
She could turn, drill or tap
Without any mishap
But at speed - well, she just 'also ran'.

There was a young lady named Jane
Went out in the wind and the rain;
Being small and petite
She was blown down the street
But she bobbed up serenely again!

Said a cheerful young lady named May
It's monotonous here every day;
And I don't like the work
But I am not going to shirk
Though I'd far rather go out and play!

There was a young lady named Carrie
Who vowed that she never would marry;
But one day to her joy
She found such a nice boy
And an old maid no longer she'll tarry!

There was a young lady named Rosie
Who always seemed tired and dozy;
But she perked up all right
When the tea came in sight
For a cup made her cheerful and rosy

Hazel Brown used to sing in the choir
Her voice it rose higher and higher
Till at last the top note
Shot clean out of her throat
And it cracked all the bells in the spire.

There was a young lady named Vera
When she talked, t'was a pleasure to hear her;
She'd have been all the rage
Had she gone on the stage
As for eloquence no one came near her.

There was a young lady named Jean
An expert at bench and machine;
There isn't a doubt
That the work she turned out
Was some of the best ever seen.

There was a young lady named Grace
Drilled holes at a terrible pace;
When the drill spindle broke
She exclaimed 'its no joke!
It'll put me clean out of the race'.

There was a young lady named Edie
Endeavoured to work very speedy;
She turned valves in galore
But the Shop Foreman swore
When he found some that looked very seedy.

There was a young lady named Lizzie
The grinder's high speed made her dizzy;
So she changed with Doreen
On the hacksaw machine
And its wheel speed was not quite so whizzy!

In fact what he said to the staff that first day (there were 15 men and boys as well as the girls) might serve as an object lesson in industrial relations.

Pay was to be on an hourly basis, with a bonus on any thing that passed the viewer. Curly arranged for a motherly young woman to see that if any girl felt ill she was not to go on working, but take a rest either in the girls' room or at home, without question. A cup of tea was to be had at any time. Similar provision was made for the men and boys; and there was no abuse.

Since it was realised that boys on repetition work are as restless as the proverbial cat on hot bricks, they were allowed to change over with someone else on another job. Curly also offered (rather pointedly perhaps) to repair alarm clocks for anyone who was late.

There was an excellent group of modern centre and capstan lathes, plus a large number of others that made the new manager feel like bursting into tears. Some of the best of them were made workable and others sent to the scrapyard they should have been sent to in the first place. Like diamonds amongst the dross were three of those famous tiny Drummond 3½in. lathes, better known to model than to production engineers; these were adapted and served very well in turning out small screws, very small bronze and cast-iron bushes, headed steel pins etc., etc., all to extremely close tolerances and by the thousand.

He tells us also how one of the dubious larger lathes was adapted for mass-production of bronze bushes at a time when all the better machines were occupied. After describing how a home-made collet chuck and lever operated tailstock arrangement was fitted, he went on to say...

'Home workers who spend an evening reaming a cylinder bore, and then get it bell-mouthed or taper, plus a bore that is anything but glass-like, should have seen Gwendolen Valerie (alias 'Tiddles') reaming bushes with the above rig-up. As she slid a bush into the collet with her right hand, her left would seek the drawbolt handle, and at the instant the bush bottomed in the collet, a deft flick of the drawbolt handle locked it. As her left hand reached for the belt striker, her right grabbed the lever of the tailstock, and ere the reamer had performed the 'in-and-out-nonstop' movement, her left hand again was on the handle of the cross-slide, moving up the tool to face off the end of the bush, the split second after the reamer left it.

'It was through 'Tiddles', incidentally, that the tool-brooch fashion started. I had made the facing tool out of a bit of carbon steel, when first setting up the machine, and the tempering colours were unusually vivid. 'Tiddles', on seeing it exclaimed, 'What pretty colours - just like a rainbow,' which, of course, it was. Several times I saw her peering closely at the tool, so I took a short length of ³⁄₁₆ square silver steel, polished it on the buff, ground the end to a miniature facing tool and heated it to reproduce the colours. I then attached it to a small safety-pin, and give it to her as a 'trade-mark' to stick on her overall. She was as delighted as if it had been a thousand-guinea diamond brooch - and within two days practically every girl in the shop was wearing a miniature replica of the tools on her machine made up as a brooch. I suppose the toolmaker and I spent about an hour, all told, for those who could not make their own. Silly? Ah, maybe you think so. If you do, you have a lot to learn about human nature.'

But in the end there came the eleventh hour of the eleventh day of the eleventh month and Curly found himself at the wheel of his yellow Tin Lizzie driving round normally sleepy Weybridge; a boy was sitting on the bonnet playing a cornet and six blue-overalled girls packed charabanc fashion in the open back were singing at the top of their voices.

Of his personal life during the war almost nothing is recorded; indeed, the munition shop was a 15 hours-a-day, 7 days-a-week task. One thing has come down to us, though; a receipt for 33 guineas for a piano, a 10-year anniversary present for Mabel. It came from a gramophone and piano dealer called Brinsmead Gough of Streatham.

Soon enough Curly was back at his pre-war job, but supplementing this by repairing gramophones for Mr. Gough. And, yes, as well, building locomotives for various client-friends. He still had his scenic outfit and one Christmas set it up and ran it in the window of Mr. Gough's shop; of this more later.

To test these locomotives he made a straight track raised on posts. In the garden at Norbury there was only room for 60 feet but this Norbury Light Railway became a line on which history was made. The drive-yourself idea swept away any thought of another elaborate scenic line; several clubs had similar set-ups in larger gauges but any 2½in. gauge locomotive that hauled live passengers was regarded as a freak. So the stage was set for 'L.B.S.C.', now waiting in the wings, to make his spectacular entrance...

The far reaches of the Norbury Light Railway seen from the top floor of 'Ellesmere'.

Chapter Four

The momentous events which became known as the battle of the boilers were very much a turning point in Curly's life. When it was joined in 1922, he was like most people earning his daily bread in a job which brought to him few rewards besides a wage packet; when it ended 2½ years later he was established as one of the top professionals in the quite small world of model engineering. As we shall see, the task of teaching people to build small locomotives remained his job and his life until the day he died.

The first shot was fired early in 1922 when there came a moment when Curly felt unable to keep silent any more about his experimenting with small steam locomotives. Some instinct told him it was the moment to reveal what he had discovered, viz., that far better results were possible than the then accepted state-of-the-art allowed. His letter was published in the Model Engineer for 9th February, 1922 and read as follows:-

Water Tubes or Fire Tubes?
TO THE EDITOR OF *The Model Engineer*

Dear Sir, - In reply to Mr. James Leeming's query re ½-in. scale locomotive fitting, as a model-maker of twenty years' experience I should advise him to scrap his water-tube boiler and put in a proper locomotive type boiler with a charcoal fire. If he does the job properly he may then have the pleasure of starting his locomotive with 20 lbs. pressure and seeing it *rise* to 100 lbs. while the engine is running.

The water tube boiler (or 'Smithies' boiler, to give it its correct title - why is not Mr. Fred Smithies given credit for his design? I well remember his single-wheeler 'Don', the first engine fitted with this boiler) - owes its popularity chiefly to its ease of construction, both amateur and commercially; but, while all very well in its way, after all it is only really an externally-fired 'pot' boiler inside a circular casing; and while most of this type are fair steamers, they are very inefficient. The amount of methylated spirits used up to burn the paint off the casing and otherwise waste heat must be enormous; and some designers, realising this, have tried to 'work-in' a water space outer shell.

The locomotive type boiler is far more difficult to construct it is admitted; but when properly made it well repays the trouble. Very little of the heat put into it is wasted, the fire being surrounded with water, practically; and there is no trouble about paint burning off, also the engine does not get so frightfully hot all over. I know some model makers have discarded the locomotive type for the water-tube - Mr. Averill, for instance; but his trouble was chiefly caused through leaking, and he admitted that his locomotive type boiler when tight was a better steamer than the water-tube, although he uses two blowlamp burners with the latter, if I remember rightly.

For my own part I have experimented with both types years ago on the same engine, with the net result that I build only locomotive type boilers. I am fitting one now to the 'Brighton Atlantic' ½-in. scale chassis shown on Bond's stand at the Exhibition.

If Mr. Leeming saw a solid-fuel model locomotive going round an outdoor line in the dusk of the evening, with the glow from the half-open fire-hole door shining brightly, the safety valves hissing and the sparks shooting up out of the chimney as high as the garden fence, it would make him want to put his methylated spirits and water tubes in the dustbin!

Faithfully yours, 'LBSC'

(James Leeming had earlier written of his disappointment with the performance of a commercial spirit-fired model locomotive - a six-wick Great Central Railway 4-6-0).

In late years Lawrence stated that this was the first occasion on which the famous pseudonym 'L.B.S.C.' was used, but this is not so. A fortnight earlier, 'L.B.S.C.' had described a scenic layout of No. 2 (2in.) gauge, then quite a popular size, which he set up as a pre-Christmas display in the shop-window of that piano and gramophone dealer, Mr. Brinsmead Gough of Streatham. On this railway there ran an LNWR 2-4-2T, an LB&SCR 'E-class' 0-6-0T and his LB&SCR 'Jumbo' 0-6-0 No. 430, the one on which he had discovered the value of early cut-off on small locomotives. All were of Curly's build; it is not possible to identify the 0-6-0T definitely with the one described in the 'Lylia' article of 10 years earlier.

The battle raged over all the technical, economic and aesthetic aspects of the comparison between water-tube and loco-type boilers. One might sum up what was said by saying that the latter (coal-fired) was accepted as costing several times the former (spirit-fired) to build, either in effort or cash, but costing only a fraction of the amount to run. Aesthetically, it became generally agreed that it was more correct to build model locomotives with the same type of boiler that big sister had; on the other hand, again rather obviously, there was no serious argument that spirit-firing was, in principle anyway, more realistic for long non-stop runs without human intervention on a scenic railway.

This general agreement on economics and aesthetics was not accompanied by similar agreement on the capabilities of the respective types. LBSC suggested that a reasonable load which a four-coupled 2½. gauge coal-fired express locomotive might be expected to haul continuously without losing pressure, was at the minimum, one substantial adult, say 170lb. (Curly's weight at this time was around 12 stone). With the commercial spirit-fired locomotives of the day, any one that could maintain pressure whilst hauling ten tinplate carriages, viz. a load of 30lb., would be regarded as remarkable. That it should be a normal thing to drive oneself and haul living loads in 2½in. gauge was a new and startling idea and, incidentally, one that totally cancelled out any superiority in realism achieved by having a real coal-fired locomotive type boiler. But on the whole it was more fun.

In the light of subsequent events and the legends that have grown up around them it is strange to find Henry Greenly and Lawrence more or less on the same side in this decisive battle. Other names that appear are Barnard (of Bassett-Lowke's), Coates, Conybeare, "Crankpin", Crook, Gowlland, Harris, "Linkhead", Peek, H. Smith, Tyrell, Wolverton, Woodrow.

Percival Marshall congratulated the participants on their straight fighting; his blue pencil was hardly needed, personal attacks being conspicuous by their absence. One regrets to record that the only sour note was from someone who should have known better; W. J. Bassett-Lowke cast doubts on Curly's veracity, in the light of a claim to have pulled two living men (a load of approximately 350lb) with his 2½in. gauge L.B.S.C.R. Brighton 4-4-2. The claim was endorsed by such unimpeachable witnesses as W. B. Hart and J. C. ('Uncle Jim') Crebbin but, even so, Curly never forgave Bassett-Lowke. In correspondence 30 years and more later both the firm and the man were still referred to as 'Bally-Joke' and in no

kindly manner either. Like the kindly gentle elephant, Curly never forgot an injury.

Bassett-Lowke could hardly be blamed for a little general suspicion of claims in the correspondence column. Even amongst the contributors to the discussion was one called himself 'Linkhead' who described taking one of his large fleet of Bassett-Lowke steam locomotives - in fact, a North Eastern Railway '796 class' 4-4-2 then advertised at £38. 10s. 0d - and coupling up 27 bogie coaches behind her. These coaches had, he said, previously been filled with a carefully weighed-out man's weight of 13 stone (180-lb) of gravel. The whole caravan was then sent off on a ¾-mile journey to the other end of his railway; finally, a second (unspecified) locomotive was despatched to bring the train back. For Bassett-Lowke this serious 'over-claim' was as bad as criticism, even when it turned out that the letter concerned was just a well-written piece of fiction.

Curly, however, did not over-claim and publicly demonstrated his unfinished and by now quite famous LB&SCR Atlantic (it was some time later that she received the name *Ayesha*) before the Society of Model & Experimental Engineers at a meeting held at the Caxton Hall, London on 19th July. This really was the turning point and shortly afterwards Lawrence wrote his first locomotive construction article for the M.E., describing how to make a coal-fired boiler with wide firebox similar to *Ayesha's*. It appeared in the issues dated 19th and 26th April, 1923; the introduction read as follows:

As a preface to these notes on the construction of a ½in. scale solid fuel loco-type boiler, the writer wishes to state that for many years past he has experimented with all kinds of boilers - 'pot', water-tube, loco, flash, and combinations of different types - and has also tried practically every method of firing. He therefore does not offer an untried design. As a schoolboy of thirteen, in the beginning of 1895, he successfully ran out

old 'Ajax' toy loco outdoors, with a charcoal fire, and, incidentally, discovered for himself the supreme importance of a good blast. It is of little use recounting here the method adopted, as these 'models' of our childhood days are only known to the older readers of the M.E., and are long since extinct; but if any reader should be interested, details are available. The result of all the experiments amply proved that for an unfailing supply of high pressure dry steam to feed big cylinders under every condition of locomotive working, a correctly designed multitubular loco-type boiler, fired by solid fuel, could not be approached (let alone beaten), providing the blastpipe and chimney were properly proportioned, the smokebox airtight and the grate bars correctly spaced. The devotees of the 'water-tube' boiler - this term being purposely used, as Mr. Fred Smithies' temper would have suffered a severe strain had he seen some of the awful atrocities perpetrated in his name - claim extreme simplicity of construction for that particular type.

However, when all is said and done, any amateur can, with a little care and patience, build a successful solid-fuel loco-type boiler if he is put on the right road; and it is to the less experienced amateurs who like a fully detailed description that the writer respectfully offers these notes. The boiler described is the one fitted to the writer's Brighton 'Atlantic' engine, which will *maintain* a working pressure of 90 to 100lbs. while supplying cylinders $1\frac{1}{16}$ in. bore $1\frac{1}{16}$ in. stroke, hauling a 200-lb load with the feed pump on all the time; this is a 'facer' for our professors of theory who prove by *figures* that such things are impossible. It will also raise steam from all cold in from five to six minutes. These are no freak performances; other boilers built to this design by other loco builders have given similar results.

At regular intervals there then followed other miscellaneous articles covering other related matters, such as the construction of a Great Western narrow-firebox boiler (9th August) or the procedure for testing a boiler (11th October). This second boiler was one which Curly had fitted to a GWR Star class 4-6-0 *Princess Mary*, built for a Mr. Tye who lived in East London.

PRINCESS MARY (2½ in gauge) had the four cylinders and inside Walschaerts valve gear of her famous Great Western 'Star' class prototype.

◀ *AYESHA needs no introduction as the worlds first 2½ in gauge locomotive to haul living adult passengers. Demonstrations of her powers resulted directly in Curly being asked to contribute his weekly series in the Model Engineer. Similarly a full construction serial marked LBSC's debut in English Mechanics six years later. AMY, a gauge 1 version of AYESHA, was described in the Model Engineer at the same time. The original AYESHA is now in the care of Mavis Harriott.*

None of this prevented our friend from tilting at various windmills in the correspondence columns; all this just came bubbling out - it was a gusher certainly and without doubt the Model Engineer had struck oil. But before this well of talent came into controlled and regular - but even greater - production, there was still to be one more happening; one, alas, that should have been just a bit of fun but which, in fact, turned out to be a source of divisive bitterness that even to this day separates the pundits of the model engineering world.

With hindsight it would seem that both Bassett-Lowke and Greenly recognised rather belatedly that the humble Curly represented a real threat to their respective supreme positions in the 'commercial' and 'model engineering' sides of small steam locomotive building. Ernest Steel (in his biography of Henry Greenly) describes his father-in-law referring a little contemptuously to 'a young man called Lawrence'. In fact, of course, Greenly and Curly were almost contemporaries and moreover the latter had (as we have seen) a formidable array of experience that suited him ideally to teach the common man to build better small steam locomotives than had ever been built

before. Also there was Curly's quite remarkable mental equipment and, as well as that, the fact that at this time he had recently become unemployed and so has no distractions such as being consulting engineer to large 15in. gauge projects.

Anyway, a challenge bout was arranged to be held at the 1924 Model Engineer Exhibition. For this, Bassett-Lowke had built especially in their works a large and handsome 3-cylinder spirit-fired 2-8-2 with water tube boiler; the locomotive was appropriately called *Challenger*. The formidable resources of that famous firm made an excellent job of a special Henry Greenly design.

In opposition, Curly first fielded a large four-cylinder 4-6-2 which he irreverently called *Maggie*, short for *Magnum Opus* (his customer, a Mr. Kirk, called her *Vindictive*). Maggie was based on the drawings which headed the Pertinent Paragraphs column in the Railway Magazine then and for many years after, but even this impeccable ancestry did not prevent her entry being disallowed on the grounds that her vital statistics exceeded the British loading gauge. So *Ayesha* stepped in to the breach.

By making this objection, Bassett-Lowke and Greenly to some extent played into Curly's hands. This was because, instead of the contest being between two well-matched opponents, it became a David and Goliath affair. In the event, then, the fact that both contestants met the requirement (of hauling a live driver for 15 minutes continuously on the S.M.E.E. up and down track) it was a victory for little 4-4-2 Ayesha, which weighed 18lb, over 2-8-2 *Challenger*, which turned the scales at 40lb, including extra lead ballast. There were one or two points of difference, but on the whole they cancelled out. For example, *Challenger* ran a slightly

VINDICTIVE was 'LBSC's' 2½ gauge four-cylinder Magnum Opus of 1923, irreverently known as Maggie by her builder. She was based on the heading of the 'Pertinent Paragraphs' feature in the Railway Magazine.

longer distance but *Ayesha* hauled a much heavier load; *Challenger* had the advantage of a hand-operated water pump instead of an axle-driven one, while *Ayesha* was a well run-in machine and accordingly less stiff.

Curly nearly spoilt his case with a note full of excuses - not all of them relevant - for *Ayesha* being half a lap behind *Challenger*. He might better have rested his case on the fact that he weighed 12 stone, while Bassett-Lowke's driver weighed only 9 stone. Even so, the natural sympathy of the crowd for David in preference to Goliath gave him a popular victory. There was also the point that a man with a treadle lathe in a backroom (with whom the average model engineer might well be able to identify) had done better than what was thought to be the most celebrated model steam locomotive manufactory in the world; although in fact B-L imported much of their stuff from Germany.

Henry Greenly, of course, had a client and in his defence published a picture of the locomotive and 470 wagons arranged in tiers, entitled 'What the "Challenger" Ought To Pull'. There were also a lot of figures, even fewer of them relevant than Curly's. In comparability terms the significant paragraph reads..........

In the allotted time the spirit-fired locomotive made 23 laps while the solid-fuel engine performed 22½ similar trips. The spirit-fired engine maintained its steam although the engine has a larger capacity and smaller wheels. Nominally the amount of steam to be supplied to the cylinders of the two engines is as follows, consideration being taken of the three cylinders and the small driving wheels of the Challenger 2-8-2 type engine -

Proportions of Steam Consumed.....

Spirit-fired loco 'Challenger'	115.0 units
Solid-fuel loco LBSC Atlantic	45.0 units

This is borne out by the respective maximum tractive efforts observed, which were 4lbs for the 'Atlantic' and 8lbs for the three-cylinder spirit-fired engine. The satisfactory point for the advocates of spirit-firing was that steam was maintained in the 2-2-8-2 type engine. The writer asked Mr. Bassett-Lowke to consider fitting a solid-fuel boiler to the same engine but his reply was that as the model maintained the full pressure of steam to the end, gave no trouble and required no attention during the run or in steam raising, he considered the arguments he had all along made were proved.

Mabel Lawrence and Vindictive at the terminus of the original Norbury Light Railway.

One sympathises with Greenly in having to make bricks without straw in this way - by selling a steam 'consumption' more than double that of a rival as a virtue. Incidentally, figures for fuel consumption provided no sensible basis for any deductions; one judge (Percival Marshall himself) said *Challenger* had consumed a pint of spirit, while another judge, (Henry Greenly, who combined the roles of judge and judged), said the figure was half that. As regards *Ayesha*, all we know is that she consumed 'a good big handful' of coal! Bassett-Lowke had one further, 'absolutely final statement' to make (on 21st February) which was really a pat on the back for himself in building such a wonderful locomotive combined with an excuse that 'our standard scale models ... (are only) designed for scale loads, not for exhibition hauling tests'. He ended condescendingly by..... 'we contend that the recent tests finish the argument altogether. In doing this we do not wish to detract from the excellent work from time to time produced by your numerous amateur contributors - Yours faithfully, For and on behalf of Bassett-Lowke Ltd., W. J. Bassett-Lowke, Managing Director'.

Perhaps Curly was a trifle naive to expect friendly fair play and sportsmanship over what was a really big business affair - but whether or not this was so he certainly never forgot or forgave those up against whom he had found himself. Indeed he was constantly to remind his thousands of readers, during the years to come of the less creditable aspects of his rivals' conduct of the affair. In view of the enormous success that was to come to him out of this episode it was a rare ungenerous act on the part of a kindly and generous man. Greenly, of course, also went on to great things but in the larger sizes, while Bassett-Lowke were to produce themselves scale-model electrically-driven locomotives in O gauge, whose quality and performance had no dubiety.

After all that had occurred, both Model Engineer and LBSC were snowed under with requests for information from people wanting to do likewise. So it should be no surprise that there came a day when Curly was invited to the M.E. Offices in Farringdon Street, London, to discuss with Percival Marshall and Walter Runciman a weekly series on steam locomotives and all that appertains to their construction and running. The first of the previous articles, those describing *Ayesha's* boiler, were written very competently in traditional third-person style, but subsequent ones had been written in what became Curly's own special colloquial manner - written, in fact, just as he might have spoken. He had apparently little difficulty in persuading these two 'Knights of the Blue Pencil' that his own way was the best. So 'Shops, Shed and Road' was born, heralding an unbroken series of articles which were to run virtually continuously for the next 35 years. They were wise, intimate, gritty, practical, instructive, often very very funny and were to be the source of immense pleasure and inspiration to thousands - as well as of chagrin to a few.

18th September 1924 was the memorable day on which Curly presented his Statement of Intent to his public as follows:-

Shops, Shed and Road
A Column of Live Steam
By LBSC

Introductory

Well, brother loco men of the M.E., after the publication of my letter on 'Loco Correspondence' recently, you can guess how surprised I was to receive 'orders' from Superintendent Marshall to book on for a non-stop run through these pages. So here we are; and before I notch up and settle down to it, perhaps it would be well to say a few words on the new route we shall 'run our train' over. We puff out of the terminus, leaving our old friends 'Messrs. Theory and Orthodox' on the platform, along with their drawing-boards and text-books, for although I shall call in the aid of drawings to illustrate various subjects that may come along from time to time, there will not be much 'paper designing' on the old lines. 'Designs' there will be, but such will be composed of the results of actual experiences of locomotive building and operating both by myself and friends, and I shall make due acknowledgement where necessary. I hate writing - would sooner make a small locomotive or work a train with a big one than write about either, so whatever slips in diction that may occur, please remember that I am a loco man first and always, and *never will make a journalist.*

Our Subjects

These come within the whole range of locomotive work, from ⅜th in. gauge to 5ft.6in. gauge. I am beginning to object to the term 'model', and in this I am not alone by a long way. We have entered on an entirely new era of small locomotives, as Driver McCullough, of Belfast and County Down line, very truly points out. The 'big' loco superintendent builds his engines to do a certain job on the 4ft. 8in. gauge, or whatever it may be; those of us who build engines for *work* and not show, have the same object in view, only our gauge is 2½ins or thereabouts. The engine which hauls a solitary passenger up and down the garden is just as much a locomotive - except in point size - as its big sister hauling the Cornish Riviera. So, therefore, we will talk about various points in the construction and operation of 'small' locomotives of all type and gauges, and describe such things as coal-fired O-gauges, working

injectors, snifting valves, steam sanding gear and lots of other gadgets, for 2½in. gauge engines and so on. Don't forget that Superintendent Marshall keeps a big report book at Farringdon Street, and it is up to you to put your complaints down in it. If we can help you, so well and good; if we cannot, well, there is no harm done. By way of varying the proceedings, I propose also to include what the 'society press' calls 'news and gossip' about railway matters large and small, and also put on record what the enginemen's parliament - 'the drivers' lobby' - thinks about matters in general. So much for that.

In the first numbers, he had to deal with urgent but miscellaneous matters raised by correspondents, but attention was also given to how-to-do-it instruction for various parts of a locomotive, beginning with the most important, a safety valve for the boiler. The famous 'George Washington' ('I cannot tell a lie') water gauge appeared on 16th October and few would argue that this is the second most important thing on a locomotive.

What might be called the anti-LBSC lobby were (indeed are) apt to dismiss him entirely as regards an engineering or scientific approach to problems. For example, Ernest and Elenora Steel (in *The Miniature World of Henry Greenly*) say ... 'On one side were the supporters of LBSC ... on the other side were the engineers and technicians who approached model engineering in precisely the same scientific manner as would be expected in full-size practice'. It is true that Curly was not a great figurer, but he was certainly very sound when it came to engineering and scientific *principles*. The failure of his rivals to apply even the simplest of them to clementary problems made it very easy for LBSC to make, quite effortlessly, apparently staggering improvements. The George Washington water gauge was a case in point; by making the steam and waterways bigger (instead of smaller) than the bore of the glass he made a water-gauge that, unlike virtually all the then existing small water-gauges, actually told the truth about the water level in the boiler. His fitting instructions began ... 'take old Ananias off your boiler and throw him in the dustbin...'!

Another thing that was handed to Curly on a plate was his improved valve-setting. Although Henry Greenly certainly knew all about the need for lap-and-lead, early cut-off for locomotive valve events, and, indeed, applied the principles very brilliantly to many of his locomotives, he did have a mistaken idea that such things were irrelevant for small models. He held to this until the end. In his own words, as published in the Model Engineer as late as 11th September, 1941, he says....

'To talk of expansion of steam in model cylinders is pure rubbish. The ⅜th in. diameter takes at least five times the normal 100 per cent cylinder-full at every stroke. The well-known 'missing quantity' is responsible for the loss. At the same time a certain accuracy is necessary, but it does not matter whether there is 100 per cent or 25 per cent cut-off, the consumption of steam will be the same. Most likely it will be much more, where the cut-off is fixed at 25 per cent of the stroke instead of working at full fear. Expansion of steam carried to excess only leads to losses in cylinder condensation.'

The idea was based on the quite reasonable premise that if you reduce the dimensions of a cylinder by one-half, the volume goes down to one-eighth of what is was, but the surface area (on which the heat dissipation depends) to only one-quarter. But for some reason he seems never to have made the very easy experiment needed to test what seemed at first rather unlikely. So Curly's very unsophisticated experiments with his Greenly-designed L.B.S.C.R. 0-6-0 (as described in Chapter 2) gave him a very easily won advantage.

The 'engineers and technicians' opposition got a present from Curly when, during this dissertation on valve events he recommended the lead of a slide valve in 2½in. gauge to be 'the thickness of a tram ticket'. The figures brigade were loud in ridicule; but this writer, who read 'Mechanical Sciences' at Cambridge University, was taught there (a) that measurements should only be as accurate as they need to be, because accuracy is expensive and too much is wasteful; and (b) that the methods must suit the means. On this basis Curly gets higher marks for scientific approach than his more highly lettered opponents, because expansion and contraction, wear and tear etc., make nonsense of any more accurately specified dimension here. Also, of course, the people he was writing for were more likely to have a tram ticket handy than a set of feeler gauges. Nowadays of course, the reverse is true and in his later days LBSC did not perhaps recognise this fully.

His injector for 2½in. gauge (the first ever for so small a scale as this) appeared on 13th November and perhaps we should applaud his scrupulousness in awarding credit where due..........

Injectors

Why is it, I wonder, that the average small loco builder regards an injector as a strange and mysterious contrivance only to be approached with awe and reverence? It *is* so; and even some 'big' enginemen are a little hazy about an injector's interior and class it along with Westinghouse donkeys, Wakefield lubricators, and such-like oddments as things best left to the tender mercies of the running-shed staff. Perhaps there is some excuse for the maker of small engines, owing to the scanty amount of available information on the subject, and therefore I hope these notes will be the means of helping those willing to carry out the job 'if they knew how'. I claim nothing special for my injectors - I am only running through a section already traversed by Mr. James Crebbin, Mr. Ferreira, and the late Mr. Henry Lea. To these gentlemen, I believe, the credit of the pioneer work is due; my humble share consists of once more upsetting an 'impossible' theory, and making a little gadget suitable for feeding the boiler of a 2½in. gauge locomotive. I hope before long to produce one much smaller still; and with that and a wide range of working pressures we may soon consign the hand-pump to limbo. Good job too!

I have chosen this pattern for description as I believe it to be Mr. Crebbin's favourite and is about the easiest to construct; also once set, it never gets out of adjustment.'

By now LBSC had really got into his stride; self-confidence was enabling him to deploy his amazing literary talents to best advantage. Listen to his Christmas message that first year, well worth quoting in full......

'As by the time these lines appear in print we shall be well into the festive season, I want you all to imagine we are at the big reunion dinner. Our worthy superintendent is in the chair, and many guests are present. The inner man has been satisfied, the cigars passed around, and the toast of 'The King' duly honoured. Now the chairman bangs his hammer and the buzz of conversation dies down as in the far corner a figure - unconventional and somewhat careworn - rises. It is LBSC himself; listen what he has to say.

'Mr. Superintendent, officers and brother loco men, it is with much pleasure that I rise to propose the toast of the evening, but before doing so I would like to say a few words bearing on the subject. You all know me for a 'firebrand' who in his column in our paper spared neither friend nor foe, and this has been the subject of much criticism both commendatory and adverse. Well, there was a method in my madness, and I should like to tell you all what my motive was, as I feel sure you will all understand me a great deal better than hitherto. Let me draw a parallel. Twenty years ago the L.G.O.C. had a huge fleet of horse buses which had undergone a little improvement since the days when Shillibeer, I think it was, put his first 'bus on the road. Suddenly a phantom arose in the shape of a motor bus and it was swiftly followed by several more. Still, the old company in its complacency took no heed, but continued on their way believing they were safe; but the motors increased, the horse 'bus passengers forsook their old servants and showered ridicule upon them for not being more up to date. At last, stung to activity, the old company threw off its lethargy, with the result that today it possesses the fine fleet and efficient service that you all know so well. So with the small locomotive. It managed to get beyond the toyshop stage, but for many years past (except in a few instances) it remained in a state of semi-stagnation. But there were some of us who wanted to see it making the same strides as its big sisters - able to burn the same fuel, deal easily with trains of twenty coaches or eighty wagons, feed its own boiler, and be in effect a 'real miniature'. I for one threw my heart and soul into the job and proved that such things were possible - but it seemed that the old 'methylated spirits and tin coach' engine was not to be ousted from its position, and even what attempts were made to produce something better proved to be full of faults. When our superintendent asked me to start the 'Live Steam' series and give my experiences, I thought what a fine chance it would give me to stir things up for the good of the small loco; to endeavour to give publicity to the faults, etc. of engines that had actually come under my notice; and to properly 'rub it in' by piling ridicule upon the inefficient or badly designed and constructed engine in the hope that in the days to come there would be 'no such thing'. Mr. Stevenson and a good many more read 'between the lines'; but now I hope you will all understand

LADY OF NARRANGASSET was an up-to-date version of a GWR 'Achilles' single. Although only 2½ gauge, steam sanding gear enabled her to haul living passengers.

that whatever I have said and done has been with one object in view, namely, the improvement of the little machine we are all so fond of.

Brother loco men one and all, I ask you to be upstanding, raise your glasses and drink to the success and prosperity of 'The Small Locomotive'. With this toast I couple the names of our worthy Superintendent, Mr. Percival Marshall, as representing the literary side; Mr. James C. Crebbin, for the Society; Mr. Fred Smithies, Mr. Bassett-Lowke and Mr. Henry Greenly (who have all 'done their bit' in the past) for the trade; and the host of small loco builders past and present who initiated the movement which brought our little friend from the toyshop, have passed it through various stages of development, and I trust will finally raise it to a pitch of perfection equivalent to that enjoyed by its big sisters of the present day.

Now, boys..........

And, as our Lancashire friends would say, 'Them's my sentiments.'

A very fine 'speech', if a trifle arrogant; but note the unkind riposte to Henry Greenly for his 'young man' remarks. Each of these men were fairly fond of making jokes at the expense of the other; but neither was at all keen on being at the receiving end. Feelings were too strong for that.

In early 1925 our hero dealt with a great variety of problems, cylinders, pumps and driving methods were notable amongst them. On 8th January there was an account of an amazing modernised GWR-type 2¼in. gauge single-wheeler *Lady of Narrangassett,* built for an anonymous client; this 4-2-2 was enabled to pull living passengers by virtue of having steam sanding gear. The latter was described in detail a fortnight later.

By mid-1925, a position had been reached that followers of Shops, Shed and Road had information to make most parts of a locomotive, from boilers to tail-lamps. What they had not yet received and were clamouring for was complete series on building

FORD PACIFIC was the subject of the first LBSC construction serial to appear; the original was built for a Mr. Joe Lozier of New York. Spirit-fired and coal-fired options were offered.

a particular locomotive from frames to tender buffers. Such serials were in time to become the main subject matter of the live steam notes. So history was made on 2nd July 1925, when LBSC offered his readers the very first instalment of the set of instructions for building the *Ford Pacific,* alias 'Florrie'.

'Florrie' was a gauge 1, Yankee style 4-6-2 with a water-tube boiler and outside Walschaerts valve-gear. On the face of it, it would seem odd that the champion of coal-fired passenger hauling should stoop to a spirit-fired job suitable for a scenic model railway as his first and so far only offering. But there were reasons; first, he was making a similiar loco for an American customer so he could be certain that the 'words-and-music' would be totally practical. Second, Curly had the power to visualize in his remarkable mind a complete locomotive with all its details, well enough to go on and build it. What he found difficult was to do the drawings. Hence it was easier for him at this early stage in his career to build first and make drawings second. Third, having never forgotten Bassett-Lowke's condescending letter, he wanted to put the ordinary amateur in a position to build a small steam locomotive of the type and size that was B-L's speciality, but which was far superior to those they imported and sold.

EILEEN was a 'Baltic' (4-6-4) tank locomotive. She was one of the first successful gauge 1 coal-burners with a narrow firebox. Curly built her for a Mr. Billyeald, but later she was sold to Mr. Calvert Holt and went to the U.S.A.

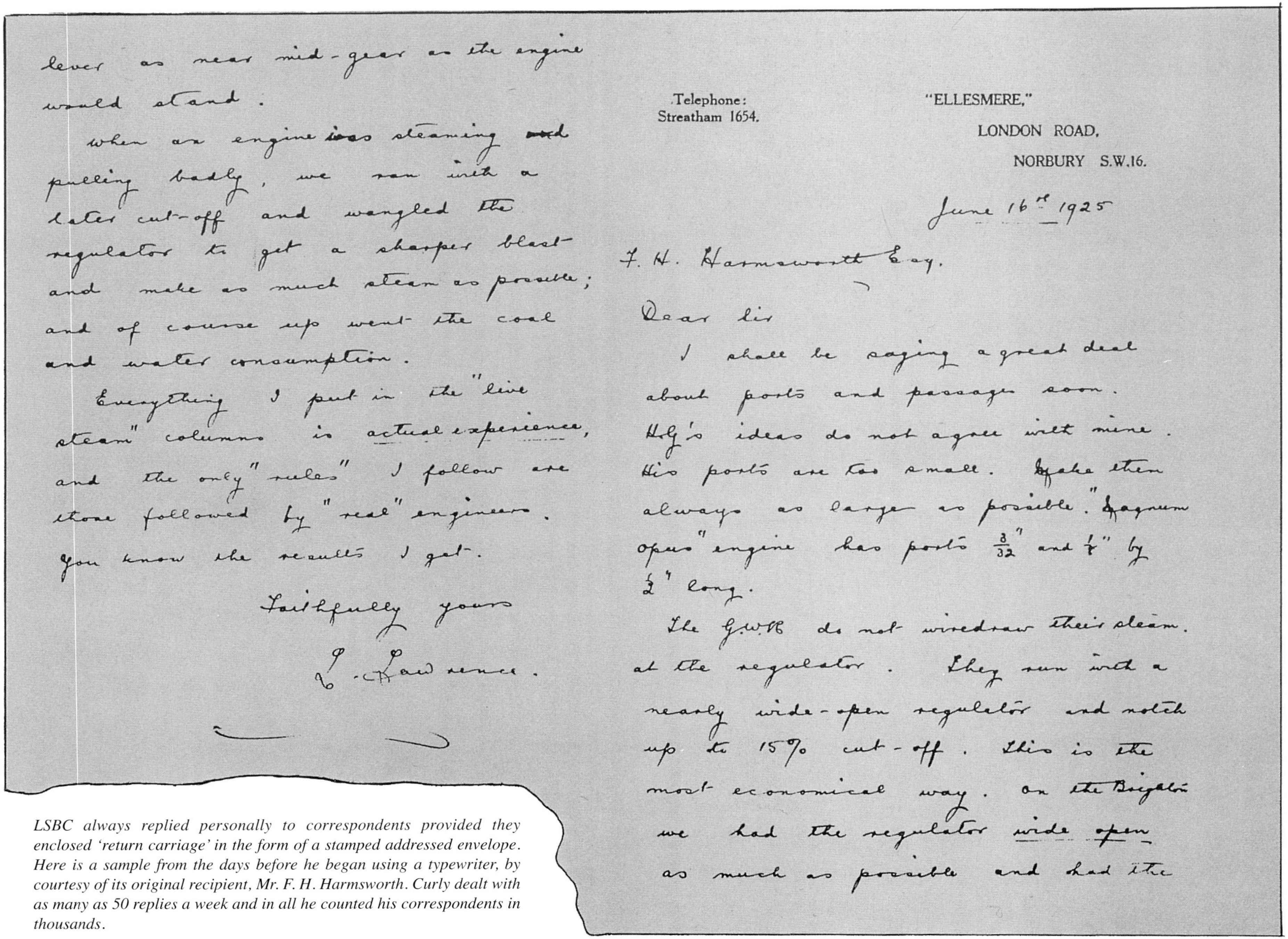

"ELLESMERE,"
LONDON ROAD,
NORBURY S.W.16.

Telephone:
Streatham 1654.

June 16th 1925

F. H. Harmsworth Esq.

Dear Sir

I shall be saying a great deal about ports and passage room. Hy's ideas do not agree with mine. His ports are too small. Spake them always so large so provide. My own engine has ports $\frac{3}{32}$ and $\frac{1}{4}$" by $\frac{3}{4}$" long.

The ... do not weaken their steam at the regulator. They run with a nearly wide-open regulator and notch up to 15% cut-off. This is the most economical way. On the ... we had the regulator wide open ... and had the ...

level as near mid-gear as the engine would start.

When an engine was steaming and pulling badly, we ran with a later cut-off and worked the regulator to get a sharper blast and make so much steam so provide; and of course so went the coal and water consumption.

Everything I put in the "Live Steam" column is actual experience, and the only "rules" I follow are those followed by real engineers. You know the results I got.

Faithfully Yours
L. Lawrence.

LSBC always replied personally to correspondents provided they enclosed 'return carriage' in the form of a stamped addressed envelope. Here is a sample from the days before he began using a typewriter, by courtesy of its original recipient, Mr. F. H. Harmsworth. Curly dealt with as many as 50 replies a week and in all he counted his correspondents in thousands.

SIR MORRIS DE COWLEY of 1926 was a passenger-hauler, the world's first for O-gauge. Sir Morris accompanied Curly on his visit to America, 'astonishing the natives' on more than one occasion.

'Florrie' hauled living loads all right, although she was intended for a scenic railway owned by a Mr. Lozier of New York; when illustrated on completion she appeared handsome but with no frills at all - hence the name. The serial was finished on 5th August, 1926, with instructions for the tender fittings. Supplementaries describing a chime whistle and sanding gear were to follow, as well as an alternative coal-firing option.

Simultaneously, another path-finding locomotive was being described; this one also was for running on a scenic line. The famous *Sir Morris de Cowley* was a Southern Railway of England-style 4-6-2, O gauge, coal-fired and (on test) passenger hauling. Sir Morris came back into Curly's hands and remained with him to the end. She is now in the possession of Mr. Deverell of London.

With all these, as well as many other distractions, it was not until

14th October, 1926 over three years after his regular M.E. contributions began, that Curly put before his public what he became famous for; viz., serial instructions aimed at beginners, for making a coal-fired passenger hauling locomotive. *Simple Sally* was based on a simple version of the North Eastern Railway 4-4-0 No. 1619, L.N.E.R. class D19. The gauge was 2½in. and the scale 1¹⁄₃₂in to 1foot. Various variations were offered, such as cylinders with valves on top instead of with valves between the frames; there was even a 4-4-2 version. Coal-firing was in fact just an option, as naturally the simplest arrangement was a water-tube boiler.

Two things detracted from the *Simple Sally* instruction; first, the author had not yet come to terms with the main difficulty of writing serials of this kind, which lies in the fact that so much of the work is repetitive. If he repeats instructions for the repetitive things, for

SIMPLE SALLY in 2½ in gauge was the first beginners' project; she was offered in a number of variations including outside or inside cylinders, coal or spirit firing and as a 4-4-0 or a 4-4-2. Provision was also made for the incorporation of finished parts; Curly's own example followed the style of North Eastern No. 1615.

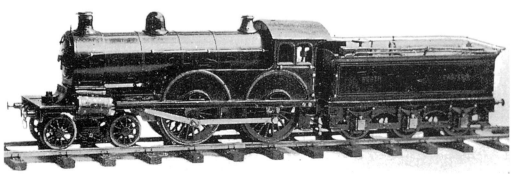

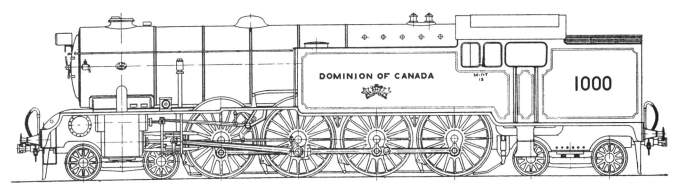

HELEN LONG was both a Curly loco and an LBSC design, his first-ever for advanced workers. The idea was that of Mr. James Joslin of Toronto for whom the original was built and this is 'J.J's' original drawing.

example boring cylinders, then regular readers also get bored. If he does not then new readers get annoyed at having to get hold of the back numbers to which reference is made. Whatever one does is wrong!

The second thing was that at this stage Curly had not learnt to sell his designs with a pithy preamble, accompanied by an eye-catching side elevation drawing; although he had already got the idea of giving a catchy name. With all this in mind it is perhaps not surprising that few *Simple Sallys* seem to have been made.

1927 brought LBSC's first elaborate locomotive design intended for experienced workers. This was the notable 3-cylinder 2½in. gauge LMS-style 4-8-4T *Helen Long*, the serial for which began in the first number of the year, illustrated by a picture of Curly's completed chassis. The coal-fired boiler had an amazing grate, 6½in. long by 1⅛th. in. wide, rather difficult to fire. In this case the side elevation was published just two years before and was the work of James Joslin, secretary of the Canadian Model Engineering Club. Joslin was Curly's customer for the engine. The *Helen* design went like wildfire and many were built.

In November, 1927 came the instructions for the first all-brazed copper boiler. Until now it was the practice for the firebox and tube assembly only to be silver-soldered; the outer seams were close riveted and then caulked with soft solder. This was a big step forward.

One of Curly's more incredible confections was brought to readers' notice in the autumn; this was his own 2½in. gauge 4-cylinder 4-12-2 *Caterpillar*, a British version of the 3-cylinder Union Pacific 9000 class. A short series on building one followed; a 3-cylinder version of *Caterpillar* was fully described in English Mechanics some years later. *Caterpillar* was another engine that

returned to Curly's possession; she is now owned by Jack Calderbank of London.

1928 was Baker Valve Gear year; it was introduced to readers on 8th March and offered to them in O gauge form as part of the works of *Minnehaha*. *Minnehaha* could be either coal or oil-fired and was a U.S.-style Atlantic locomotive made for a line in a New York flat. Then in late December came the legendary *Fayette*, an Anglo-American type 4-6-2 with Baker Valve Gear, Vanderbilt tubular tender and duplex steam donkey feed-pump masquerading as a Westinghouse brake compressor. She was quite lovely and became very popular. A photograph of Curly's own version (built for a 'client-friend') illustrated the preamble to the series. Castings, drawings and parts for *Fayette* are still on offer fifty years later, notably by Kennions of Hertford.

In mid-1929 there was time for a short series on *Lady Kitty*, a G.W.R. 47XX class mixed-traffic 2-8-0 for 2½in. gauge. Incidentally, the original Lady Kitty has recently turned up in Bristol. In 1929 he also contributed to the Model Engineer a series of articles on repairing gramophones.

Talking of the G.W.R., two very important railway officials from that line paid a personal visit to the shops of the Norbury Light Railway. Curly had got to know a certain Sir Aubrey Brocklebank, Bart., a Liverpool shipping magnate, who was a director of the Great Western Railway and chairman of its Locomotive Committee. Sir Aubrey had had no satisfaction from a collection of 2½in. gauge steam locomotives which were built for him by a long defunct Sheffield firm until several of them had been given the famous 'monkey-gland' treatment at Norbury. The result so far as Curly was concerned was that C. B. Collett, Chief Mechanical Engineer, designer of both 'Kings' and 'Castles', came to see him

MINNEHAHA was another Baker gear locomotive, this time for O gauge. Curly built her for an American customer.

BLACK BESS (2½in gauge) was a might-have-been – an LNWR 'Experiment' with a 'Claughton' sized boiler.

FAYETTE was a 2½ in gauge Anglo-American Pacific fitted with Baker valve gear. This superb example is called Victoria ('she of the stainless steel motion') and was the work of Inspector Meticulous himself, alias Tom Glazebrook who is seen at the regulator. Curly's own version had a 'Vanderbilt' tubular tender.

CATERPILLAR of 1928 was the result of one of Curly's bad headaches - a British version of the Union Pacific 9000 class 4-12-2. She was 2½ in gauge and had four cylinders with cranks set at 135o; a version with three cylinders was described in full English Mechanics later.

GREAT WESTERN RAILWAY.

C. B. COLLETT,
Chief Mechanical Engineer.

Telegrams:
LOCO. SWINDON.

Telephone:
SWINDON 185.

Please quote this reference—

56891
OT/16/4

Chief Mechanical Engineer's Department,

SWINDON, WILTS.

Saturday,   October 20th   1928.

Your reference—

Dear Sir,

I am very much obliged to you for sending me the little valve gear model, and must thank you once more for the interesting demonstration you gave me last Thursday of your latest production.

I have pleasure in enclosing you an engine pass for Saturday next from Paddington to Birmingham and back.

Out, King Ed. V.
dead stop at Bordesley
2 mins early in Snow Hill.
Back, Cleeve abbey, Ran from Banbury
to signal stop at Royal Oak, in 55 mins.

Yours faithfully,

C. B. Collett

---

in company with Sir Aubrey one memorable autumn afternoon. *Fayette* complete with Baker valve gear was run for them and the occasion was one (Curly had a certain amiable weakness for name-dropping) which was often recalled in later live steam notes.

Collett's letter of thanks is reproduced above....

Curly records travelling out on *King Edward V*, then quite new, arriving 5 minutes early Snow Hill - in spite of the almost inevitable stop at Bordesley just outside. He returned on *Cleeve Abbey*, coming up from Banbury in 55 minutes to the similar halt at Royal Oak just outside Paddington.

TALULA (2½in gauge) was described in the part-work 'Wonderful Models' in 1927.

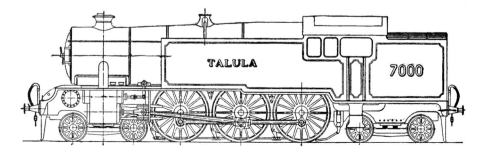

One result of this affair was election as an Associate Member of the Institute of Locomotive Engineers, to whom he read a paper on Baker valve gear the following year. He also received some inside knowledge of such Swindon secrets as the true rather than the published valve-settings on G.W.R. locomotives, Lillian Lawrence, Esq., A.M.I. Loco. E., Chartered Locomotive Engineer, had, in 30 years, come a long way from engine cleaner.

The Norbury Light Railway, on which so much history had been made, came up for abandonment in the autumn when the Lawrences had to give up the lease of their house. A developer had bought the properties near Norbury Station, with a view to making them into shops and offices. Curly fancied the idea of emigration to the United States - as the American flavour of his articles during the last year or two hinted. He had many friends and clients over there, as well as a half-promise of an engineer's (driver's) post on an American railroad. In fact they were to sail at the end of November, having given up the house a month or so earlier, they took temporary accommodation in Bromley.

LADY KITTY was both a product of the Norbury Shops and a series in the Model Engineer. She was a replica of the rare GWR '47XX' class; the original recently turned up in Bristol and is in the hands of Paul Weise.

POLLY was a commercial product which came to Curly for his celebrated 'monkey gland' treatment; after which her performance came up to the high standards set by her big sisters, the celebrated Pollitt singles of the Great Central Railway.

RIVER STYX was based on the ill-fated S. R. 'River' class express tank locomotives. She was 2½in gauge and completed in 1928.

MISS LINDY was a Curly 2½in gauger. She was based on the Lancashire & Yorkshire Railway's famous Atlantics.

CANADIAN SWITCHER in 2½in gauge was a simple design for beginners. There was also an English version.

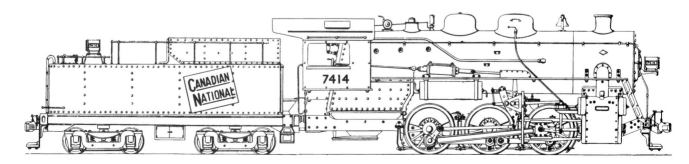

TANGO was a 2½in gauge Great Nothern-style 2-8-0 which was the first locomotive of any size in Britain to be fitted with Southern valve gear. This was in 1927.

Two views of Tango's Southern valve gear; above, in forward position; below, in reverse.

It was significant of the relationship between Curly and his admirers that they needed to know everything about his visit to America in 1929-30. Following the cataclysmic events of October 1929 on Wall Street (the United States Stock Exchange) the time was not at all propitious; whatever may have been the case when he booked his passage, by the time he arrived jobs of any kind were very difficult to come by and good ones like locomotive driving quite impossible. But it was a case of an ill wind, for he had no choice but to continue writing Shops, Shed and Road, much to our advantage back in Britain. In fact, no issue was missed when he went out, a remarkable achievement when viewed amongst the distractions of settling in a new country.

His readers had been well prepared beforehand - provided they could read between the lines to a small extent - but even so it was a shock to read the notes for 9th January, 1930 written in the saloon of a westernbound liner! But perhaps they (and Curly) took comfort that *Ayesha* and *Sir Morris* were stowed away somewhere below. November weather in the North Atlantic gave both people and locomotives aboard a rough passage. In fact the latter sustained some damage.

The Lawrences were taken under the wing of a Mr. Calvert Holt, who had visited at Norbury. Calvert Holt was a professional engineer and owned a firm called the Pierrepont Engineering Co. He lived in an exclusive residential suburb of Greenwich, Connecticut, called Milbrook; it had (and has) private roads, a private lake and a guard on the gate. People who lived there were quite wealthy. The Holts' house, 12 West Brother Drive, had about 12 rooms and it is likely that at first the Lawrences stayed there. Later Holt built them a traditional trans-atlantic frame-and-shingles house in the grounds.

Greenwich was and is a small country town situated on the mainland coast of Long Island Sound, 28 miles north of New York City. It was located on the New York to Boston main line of the New York, New Haven & Hartford Railroad, a 45-minute ride from Grand Central Terminal by overhead-electric trains.

Holt also built little steam locomotives both for himself and professionally, although this was a kind of hobby too, rather than a bread-and-butter operation. He advertised regularly in the Modelmaker, of which more later. No doubt the idea was that Curly should help him out with this and that is in fact what happened.

Curly tells of an occasion when he was brazing a boiler with Holt's huge paraffin (kerosene) blow-lamp cum flamethrower. All at once there was a tremendous shrieking noise which turned out to be the Holt's small son. He had crept in to the workshop to see what was going on, but the roar of the flames and Curly standing there with his eyes shining green like a cat's (a phenomenon that persisted with him until middle age) proved too much! It has been suggested that this is a symptom of a disease called Porphyria from which George III was a sufferer; it leads to an intermittent lack of mental balance, which would explain something of Curly's behaviour in later life, if true.

Carl Purinton, who became a big wheel for many years in the Brotherhood of Live Steamers, visited Curly at the Holts'. He remembers that Curly was too shy to look at him directly; on the other hand he was not too shy to say bluntly when Carl explained

The timber house which was the Lawrences' home in Greenwich, Connecticut, USA. The master is enjoying himself.

his ideas for the brake gear on the loco he was building . . . . 'you'd better get it to run first'.

Shortly after arrival, Curly used the then excellent train service to visit the annual exhibition of the New York Society of Model Engineers, where he met many old friends; and not only old friends, also his children. The Baltic tank *Eileen* was there, as well as *Ford Pacific* now known as 'Lizzie'. There was also a model of Stephenson's *Rocket*, which had been modified at Norbury. Little *Minnehaha* nearly got wrecked through overdoing it in her excitement. Curly also inspired the organisers to fix up a passenger hauling line and both *Ayesha* and *Ford Pacific* performed on it. The latter made the New York daily newspapers; all concerned were amazed when such a tiny machine shifted two live passengers!

Charles Small, now of Cos Cob, Connecticut, writes . .

'I joined the New York Society of Model Engineers in 1928 or 1929 at the age of 15. I well remember LBSC, for the society set up a portable track and he presided over running one of his engines. As the youngest member I was accorded the privilege of making several trips at the throttle.'

'I also recall that I had difficulty in understanding LBSC's loco driving instructions for he spoke in such a low tone of voice. You can imagine the crowd of members who had come to see this unusual event and LBSC seemed ill at ease among the throng.'

One acquaintance made at the Show, was a Mr. Vincent Astor, who turned out to be one of the richest and most powerful men in U.S.A.; the upshot was that a week or two later Curly found himself with Calvert Holt for company, rolling down the side of the Hudson River in a 1000-ton train behind a big Pacific with Baker valve gear and booster. Their destination was Rhinecliff, New York State, where Astor had his fabulous 3½in. gauge Toonerville Railroad. This was a ground level railway, full of gradients and curves and gave very nearly a mile run. From Curly's description he was in seventh heaven, in spite of December weather, driving locomotives on this most elaborate pike, complete with automatic semaphore signals, trestle bridges, switches arranged to be thrown from the trains and many other amenities. Flat cars loaded with short lengths of fullsize railroad rails could be used to make up heavy loads for test purposes.

On a later visit one of the Toonerville 4-6-2s was brought back for the fabled 'monkey gland' treatment. Further visits were paid in order to test the alterations and try out other members of the fleet. Wheels in the form of an old Ford Model T were acquired and, as we have seen, they had a nice place to live, now complete with small railroad. We know this because on 27th March there appeared in the Model Engineer an illustration of the 'reconstructed' Norbury Light Railway with that little frame-and-shingles house ('our little grey home in the West') in the back-ground, the master himself driving a 2½in. gauge Pennsylvania Railroad K4 class, a 4-6-2 appropriately called *Sylvanie*. Also in this month came the first of a new series of Live Steam Notes, which appeared in a delightful little monthly magazine called The Modelmaker, published by Spon & Chamberlain of 120 Liberty Street, New York. It is not to be confused with a short-lived British periodical called Model Maker, published after World War II, for which Curly also wrote. Since they were the New York agents of Percival Marshall & Co., Spon & Chamberlain knew all about 'LBSC'.

The series was called 'ON THE PULL-AND-GO DIVISION - Talks About Locomotives' by Mr. L. Lawrence, articles began much as Shops, Shed & Road did, with how-to-do-it articles on boiler fittings and other accessories, plus the occasional 'lobby chat'. Contributions continued until December 1931 when they stopped unexpectedly, although the article that month - on hydrostatic lubricators - spoke of dealing next with the direct-acting automatic type of lubricator. There was a gap until November 1934, a month when The Modelmaker resumed publication after a short period of 'temporary suspension due to financial conditions'. Curly managed a delightful semi-transatlantic style, as his re-introduction that month shows . . . .

'Well, brother loco-men of U.S.A. and Canada, here we are again, the older boomer hoghead-cum-back-shop-machinist-cum-roundhouse-nut-splitter has drifted back to the Pull and Go Division of the Modelmaker R.R. once more, and Master-Mechanic Spon has put my name up on the board. It is now up to you to tell him what spell of duty to call me for. The notes I write for the British journals, are chiefly guided by the correspondence received from brothers on that side of the pond, plus specialities such as the detailed instructions for building a locomotive for a silver trophy to be presented at the 1935 M.E. Exhibition in London; but here I'm to serve you, if you'll just say what you want. Here are my own ideas.

Most of you know I've got a No. 1 sized bee in my bonnet, that a little locomotive which has the appearance of a steam hog, should be a real steam hog, and not an electric gadget so darn ashamed of its motive power, that it has to doll itself up in its steam sister's clothing. The fine electric locomotives of the New York Central, Pennsy, New Haven, and other roads, must wonder what on earth is the matter with their personal appearance, that they are neglected in the small sizes. I have spoken to several builders of what I call the 'abortions' and their principal excuse is that you can't get the power in a baby steamer. I guess they've never taken trouble enough to find out. Shall we put them wise, brothers - shall I give detailed instructions how to build, say a 4-8-4 in gauge O that will not only pull the hide off any imitation coffee-mill that ever hid up an electric motor inside its fake tin boiler-barrel but give its owner a ride if he can sit safely on a flat car on such a small pike.

In the larger gauges, would you like the dope on building up a complete locomotive of any special type; or would you rather have some general notes on machining and fitting work, 'monkey-gland' valve setting (you all know what that is) or fitting yo such things as working automatic air brakes and what-have-you? Anyway, sing out; it's your call.'

A serial describing an O gauge 4-8-4 called *Lucy Anna* began in April 1935, the same month that the name of A. C. Kalmbach appears together with Francis Spon's as 'Associate Editors'. A. C. Kalmbach was the founder of magazines *Model Railroader* and *Trains* and, no doubt, he put some order into what had evidently been until now an enchanting and happy-go-lucky but perhaps a

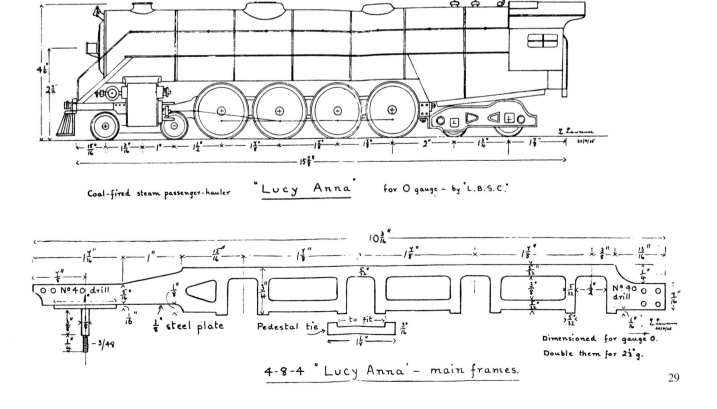

Coal-fired steam passenger-hauler   "Lucy Anna"   for O gauge - by 'L.B.S.C.'

4-8-4 "Lucy Anna' - main frames.

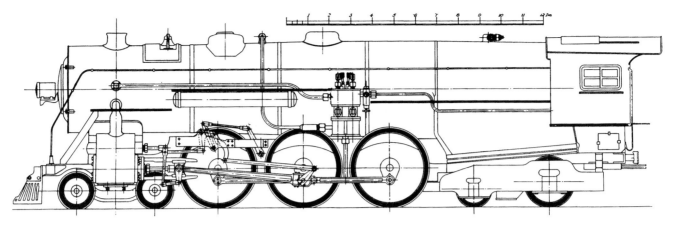

JUDY was a design for a 3½in gauge New York Central 'Hudson', published in 1930. It was a joint effort by LBSC, Calvert Holt and Fred Grimcke.

trifle unbusinesslike enterprise. By combining the July and August issues and skipping September, the October came out reasonably to time! Eventually Spon retired and administration was moved to Kalmbach headquarters at Milwaukee; Curly's last contribution appeared in June 1937. But long before all this, he had come back home.

There is a slight enigma about Curly's sudden return to England. He once told Geoffrey Cashmore that he came back because his Mother was taken seriously ill; his account of the affair to the readers describes halting his old Tin Lizzie beside a grade crossing in Pleasantville, New York, on June 15th and watching a train go by behind a New York Central 4-6-2 . . . . .

> 'I remarked to my wife, 'Wouldn't I just love to take a 3½in. gauge edition of that baby over to THE MODEL ENGINEER exhibition in September, and show 'em around the kitchen - get old Irvin to make up in the American engineer's rig-out and drive it, and smother Uncle Jim and Bill 'Art with blacks, and generally play Old Nick. Ah, well! guess we shan't see the show this year'. Yet the unexpected happened. At 4.30 the next afternoon came the fateful message that sent us scurrying across the Atlantic, and so we saw the show after all.'

One might note in parentheses that the gentlemen mentioned were all leading lights of the Society of Model and Experimental Engineers in London. His friends Hold, Lozier and others saw Curly and Mabel off from the dock in style when they sailed from New York in the *Berengaria*. They arrived in London on June 30th, slightly delayed by the fact that only three out of the liner's four turbines were working.

Since then information has come to hand that his Mother recovered, not to pass on for another twelve years, so it would seem likely that there was some other reason for his coming back to us and at this distance in time and space one can but speculate. There is no sign that he fell out with Holt, for tales of Holt's doings continued, indicating much communication between the two of them. He had found the American Way of Life very much to his taste; moreover he was recognised as the leader in his chosen vocation over there as much as he was in England. Even today reference to him and his work is frequently made in the U.S. Live Steam magazine. Furthermore, in addition to many friends, he had a sister in not-too-far-off Toronto.

It is true that his ambition of obtaining an engine-driver's position on a U.S. railroad was not fulfilled, but he was still able to continue

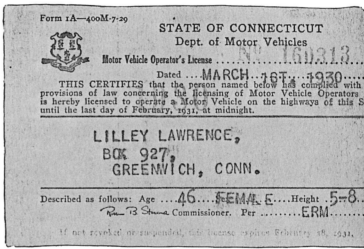

Curly's Connecticut driving licence has points of interest.

his contributions to the Model Engineer and, of course, with his reputation and connections there was small steam locomotive work to be had in America. Maybe he, or perhaps Mabel, or maybe both of them were just unbearably homesick. But whatever the reason, all of us in the Old Country must be grateful for it.

Mabel Lawrence on board R.M.S. Berengaria returning from U.S.A. in July 1930.

DAIRYMAID of 1930 for 2½in gauge was a replica of a L&SWR Drummond 4-4-0.

What is probably the true reason for never finally staying in the U.S.A. lies in the fact that Uncle Sam's immigration people might have been unhappy about Lillian Lawrence's origin as a girl. For another reason, distinguished soldier, author and railway-enthusiast John Masters had similar difficulties; he and his ancestors for several generations back had been born in India when it was part of the British Empire. Accordingly they had Indian birth certificates and Indians then had to face a wait of several years. He describes in his auto-biography Pilgrim Son how the problem was solved by the postman after some of the most distinguished names in America had used their influence to no avail; the solution was for his British-born wife to apply. Once accepted she could have a husband with her, no questions asked!

Curly's return from America in 1930 was heralded by the first issues of the Model Engineer since September 1924 not to contain any of his contributions. These were the numbers for 3rd and 10th July. Since he only landed in England on 30th June, it would appear that the distress and agitation engendered by the bad news of the 16th June had precluded his writing or finishing them in time.

On 31st July he announced his return for good, in an article which was stated to be the first to be penned on British soil - presumably those published on 17th and 24th July had been written on board ship. On 16th July he paid cash (£835) for a newly built house at 121 Grange Road, Purley Oaks, South Croydon, Surrey, which was to be his home for life, as all his fans well know.

We must salute the Lawrences in that, after all the expenses of a double journey across the Atlantic, as well as making a temporary home in a strange land, they had husbanded sufficient hard-earned resources not only to buy a house for cash, but also to re-equip the workshop. He was even able to buy a then almost unheard-of luxury (for Britain) called a refrigerator. Receipts for £56. 6s. 0d. from the Frigidaire Company's London showroom have survived - such exotic devices were in no way available from High Street shops 50 years ago. They also cost ⅟₁₅th the cost of a new house then!

SISTER DORA was LBSC's first construction series for 3¾ gauge. She was a LNWR 'Jumbo' 2-4-0, very similar to Mabel of 34 years later.

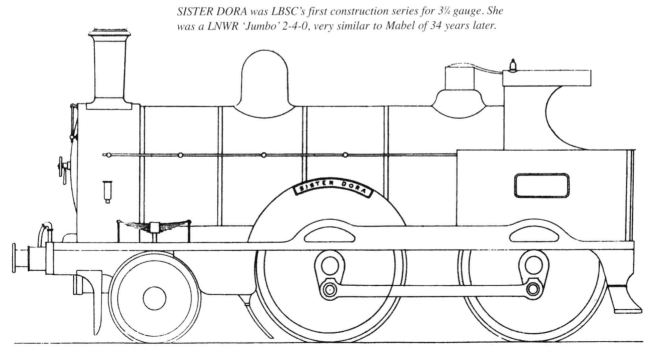

Lawrence's output of locomotive designs during the decade of the 1930s was quite prodigious. Quite often 'LBSC' would have two serials running simultaneously in the Model Engineer and a third in another weekly periodical called English Mechanics. He describes how the editor of English Mechanics met him off the boat train at Waterloo and signed him up there and then for a weekly series; this began on 8th August, only five weeks later.

The English Mechanics articles were quite different from those in the Model Engineer. In the former there appeared serial instructions for only one locomotive at one time and that, and only that, occupied the modest space allotted - usually a single page. A few dissertations on general and miscellaneous subjects bridged the gap from one serial to the next. On the one hand there were fewer distractions for a serious locomotive builder, but on the other there was not quite so much fun.

Curly opened the batting with instructions for building his evergreen *Ayesha*, to which his introduction read as follows..........

Small Locomotive Construction

Notes on the Building and Running of Small Power Locomotives

No doubt many of the readers of ENGLISH MECHANICS will recognise an old friend in the writer of these notes, but to new friends and locomotive enthusiasts it may be mentioned that he is an old engineman, who has spent the best part of his life with locomotives large and small; has helped to build and operate all sizes of engines from 4ft.8½in. gauge, down to 1¼in. gauge; and now hopes to pass on for our readers' benefit the experience gained in many years' actual work. In this series we shall be mostly concerned with the construction of locomotives of 2½in. gauge size or thereabouts, and I shall endeavour to set down full instructions how to build, run, and maintain such engines to pull heavy loads continuously at little cost. My credentials are that I built the first locomotives to burn ordinary steam coal and haul living passengers on gauge 2½in., gauge 1, and finally gauge O; the latter at Kingsway Hall, London, in 1926.

It has been suggested that I should start by describing how to build a copy of my Southern Railway Atlantic locomotive 'Ayesha'. She was the original 2½in. gauge passenger-hauler; began work in January, 1922, and has run ever since then without any heavy repairs; she has been to

America and back, working at the New York S.M.E. Exhibition and on several private roads, one of which was shown in this paper (page 329, July 11th). Her record haul was the starting of a mixed load of nine passengers, over a thousand pounds dead weight, at the Royal Horticultural Hall Exhibition, in September, 1926, with a tractive effort at the drawbar equal to the weight on the driving wheels. Anyone who builds the locomotive and puts reasonably good workmanship into it, can expect to haul at least three adults, on a good track with a free-running flat car to carry the load. The engine is very simple to build; simpler, if anything, than a 4-4-0 type, as the wide firebox boiler gives more room to work on the staying, etc. The arrangement of wheel-spacing will allow the locomotive to run around a 25ft. circle. A large and expensive kit of tools and machinery is not needed; in fact, a lathe can be done without if the turned parts are bought ready machined; but I would strongly advise all would-be locomotive builders to get possession of this useful article. If finances won't admit of much outlay, invest in a second-hand or 'part-used' one of some well-known make.

To illustrate the difference in his approach to the readers of two journals, one might look at a then recent reference in the Model Engineer to *Ayesha*; describing in fact how she got called after that lady.....

I don't know if I ever told you how she collected up that name, but it was like this. After she made her first public appearance and 'astonished the natives' by easily hauling live passengers at one of he earlier MODEL ENGINEER Exhibitions, a well-known leading light in the world of 'model' locomotives, told all and sundry that an engine on 2½in. gauge straining itself to that extent would be worn out in a week or so, and probably would fall to pieces after the Exhibition. Well, I heard all about it, so I just had a quiet laugh and said, 'Is that so? Well, we shall see. I will run her until she *does* fall to pieces, and tell everybody when it comes off.' That was January 1922. It is now October 1929. She had burned about 4cwts. of coal, had drivers of all nationalities, run goodness knows how many miles and hasn't fallen to pieces yet. Now connect up with the following.

I guess most of you have read, or anyway heard of Rider Haggard's tale 'She'. The lady's name was Ayesha, and through having a sort of patent firebath in her early days, 'stayed put' for about two thousand years without having to bother about lipsticks, face powder, or any other kind of beauty-preserver. With no night clubs, dances, cigarettes,

SMALL BASS was a narrow-gauge industrial shunter, a simple job for beginners; the design was for O and 1 gauges, as published in English Mechanics late in 1930.

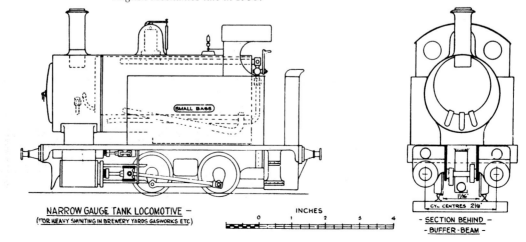

NARROW GAUGE TANK LOCOMOTIVE –
(FOR HEAVY SHUNTING IN BREWERY YARDS GASWORKS ETC)

INCHES

- SECTION BEHIND -
- BUFFER · BEAM -

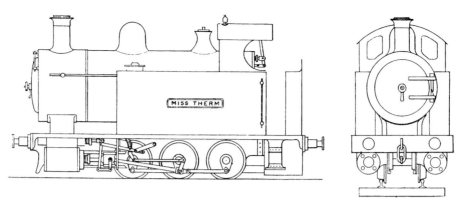

MISS THERM - slightly different from but filling the same niche as SMALL BASS in the LBSC design family.

cocktails, etc., her long life was getting a bit tame when all of a sudden she hit up against the reincarnation of her old lover, whom she had 'done in' in a fit of jealousy all those years ago. 'I better make sure of keeping him this time', she thought; and as a firebath department was still going strong, she trotted him along to sample it; but not being an engineman who has opened the firehole door without putting the blower on, naturally he felt funky. 'Well', said Ayesha, 'you're a poor sort of guy, I must say. See here now - if I go in first will you take a chance?' 'Sure', said he. 'Then right forward - all aboard!' said Ayesha; and dressing herself like Lady Godiva, she stepped right into the firebath. But she had forgotten that you can have too much of a good thing; and sad to tell, firebath No. 2 promptly cancelled out the effects of firebath No. 1 so that poor Ayesha just collapsed up into a heap of bones and dust; while her fiance, scared stiff, headed for home with a wide-open throttle. That is how the tale goes - with allowances for 'excessive condensation'!

One day the old Atlantic engine was merrily bowling up and down the N.L. in charge of a Brighton engineman friend, and I happened to mention about the 'model expert's' pronouncement, at which he laughed heartily. 'Fall to pieces - not she!', said he, emphatically if ungrammatically. 'Why, bless your soul, she'll be just like Ayesha in Rider Haggard's book - run for two thousand years before she collapse up into a heap of junk!'. Anyway, the name stuck all right, and in due course was consolidated by a pair of little nameplates on the leading splashers.

Other fun-and-games offered to Model Engineer but not to English Mechanics readers involved those enchanting characters who kept interrupting - in order to make serious technical points. There was the irrepressible Bert Smiff who would come up with remarks like 'Cor Lumme, Mate, yer chevvy chase don't 'alf need a squeeze-and-squash'. This was a comment on the important effect of over-adequate lubrication when running a small steam

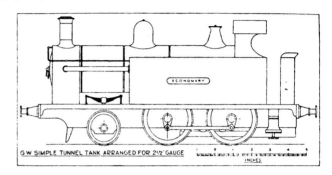

ECONOMETTE, MISS ECONOMY and ECONOMARY were respectively O, 1 and 2½ in gauge versions of the GWR 'Metro' 2-4-0Ts. Their descriptions ran in English Mechanics during 1931 and were intended as the ultimate for simplicity and quick construction.

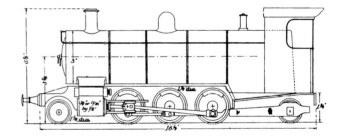

LITTLE JACK HORNER, a series published in 1931, was a narrow-gauge colonial type locomotive; it was 2½in size running on 1¾in tracks. The lower picture gives an illustration of a 'ghost crew'. The design anticipated by many years the current fashion for replicas of narrow gauge prototypes.

locomotive; if too much, spots of black oil bespatter the locomotive and driver. 'Squeeze-and-Squash', of course, is Cockney Rhyming Slang for 'wash'. Bert Smith became a fighter pilot in World War II and was killed.

Another character in the notes was Inspector Meticulous in real life a man called Tom Glazebrook, who, before he died in 1980, gave a good deal of help with this book. He was always declaring his shocked surprise at Curly's short-cut methods. A certain Noel van Raalte of Bursledon near Southampton got the name 'Bro. Wholesale', derived from his way of doing things, as we shall see in the next chapter. There was even a Bro. Nobody, derived from a habit of not signing letters!

During the 1930s, Curly offered his clients no less than 42 different designs of locomotive to build. Of this prodigious output easily the most notable was a Great Northern Railway 4-4-2 in 3½in. gauge, described in the Model Engineer between April 1935 and May 1937. The prototype was made for an LNER official called F. E. Williams (his nickname was 'Bill Massive' after the massiveness of the specifications he called for in building the locomotive. She and the series were named *Maisie* after Williams' daughter. Maisie Frost (nee Williams) writes........

'I actually met Mr. Lawrence once, when we were quite young. He paid Dad a visit, and I remembered Mother saying she was quite sure he wouldn't be interested in children; there were three of us but when he asked Dad where we were, he was brought in to see us.'

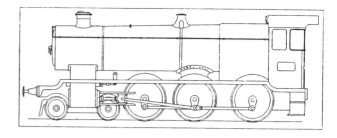

MABEL HALL, another GWR 2½ gauger, was a now almost forgotten design, published in English Mechanics during 1931. Note the raising of the boiler pitch to give more room for the firebox.

Castings and parts for this locomotive are still available; moreover, the very complete words-and-music has been reprinted in book form since the war. Unusually for Curly, the design was a super-detail one, including such extras as working vacuum brakes. It was his longest ever serial. *Maisie* was and is very popular; over forty years later one firm alone is selling an average of 20 sets of castings and materials each year. *Maisie* has also been successfully built for 10¼in. gauge, three times the size. Since the London, Brighton & South Coast Railway's Atlantics were almost identical (Locomotive Superintendent Marsh came from Doncaster), *Maisie* could also be regarded as a larger and more complex version of *Ayesha*. There was an O gauge version called *Amy* as well.

MAISIE for 3½in gauge, both as regards Curly's original and the construction serial in the Model Engineer, was one of his masterpieces. This is reflected in the fact that, not only are all the words-and-music still available in book form, but also in that numerous Maisies are still being built. Many other Great Northern Atlantics passed through Curly's hands for 'monkey-glanding' and rebuilding, TIGER and ROLAND PHILLIPS being being two examples. The photograph shows Curly's original, built for an LNER official known as 'Bill Massive' and named for his daughter.

One cuckoo in the nest was a free-lance 0-6-0 tank called *Eva May*, Curly's first for 5in. gauge, 1¹⁄₁₆in. to 1ft. scale. Today this size is more common even that ³⁄₄in., while 2½in. is now so little regarded that many club tracks do not provide the extra rail needed to provide that size. One notes in this now rare gauge the first design with derived valve gear, Sir Nigel Gresley's 2-6-2 *Green Arrow*. The valve of the inside cylinder is driven by the '2-to-1' gear designed (in the prototype) by Harold Holcroft of whom more later. *Little Jack Horner*, a narrow-gauge type locomotive equal in size to a normal 2½in. gauge one, but for running on 1¾in. gauge tracks, anticipated a current fashion by many years, but one might draw a veil over *Ugly Duckling*, a steam-driven diesel-outline abomination. LMS-type 2-6-0 *Princess Marina* and North Eastern 4-40 No. 750 *Miss Ten-to-Eight* complemented *Maisie* (which has Stephenson's valve motion) by offering, in 3½in. gauge, Walschaerts and Joy gear respectively. *Mabel Hall, Purley Grange, Kingette* and 5.15 *from the City* kept the GWR flag flying

KINGETTE in 2½in gauge was Curly's first series describing a complex scale model - a term her designer particularly disliked; she had four cylinders and full correct valve gear, of course. Cyril Grose, who took so many of the pictures which illustrated the old Live Steam Notes is seen at the regulator.

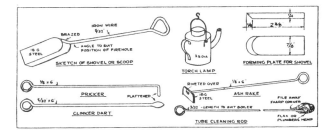

The finishing touches to a live-steam passenger-hauling locomotive were these items offered to English Mechanics readers in 1933.

BELLE STROUDLEY was an LB&SCR 'Grosvenor' single brought up-to-date. The Model Engineer ran the design as a short series for 2½ gauge.

BLUEBELL was Curly's own idea of what a Great Eastern Atlantic might have been like. She was built for a customer in 1932.

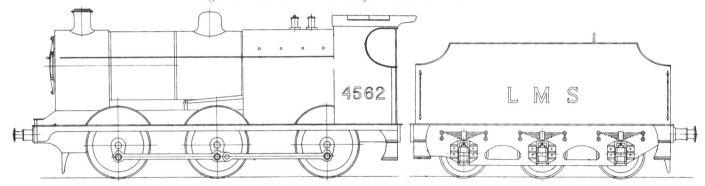

LMS 4562 was a 2½in gauge '4F' class. Long afterwards, when he had retired from writing for the Model Engineer, Curly built one of these for his own enjoyment. She was called Harriet.

Something-like-an- L&NWR 2-2-2 was NIPPY of 1932 for 2½in gauge, described in English Mechanics.

The idea of ANNIE BODDIE was that 'any body' could build her; as described in the Model Engineer for 2½in gauge during 1933. This example belongs to Mr. Fillingham.

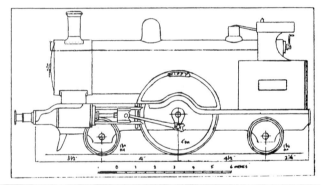

JOSIE was based on the famous New York Central 'Hudsons'. The O-gauge original was built for an American client, but a construction series appeared simultaneously in the Model Engineer.

and maybe it is significant that trans-Atlantic material was conspicuous by an almost complete absence during this aftermath of the recent adventure 'across the pond'.

Amongst a number of beginners' projects, one that stands out was this 2-6-0 *Dyak* of hybrid but quintessentially British design. Coupled with its debut on 6th September 1934 was an announcement of a prize in the form of a beautiful silver casket to be presented to the best example made by a genuine beginner, to be exhibited AND RUN at the Model Engineer Exhibition held in Autumn 1935, then barely over a year away. The trophy which was won by Mr. R.S.E. Hill of Norwich had been presented by an Englishman working in Borneo (hence the name of the locomotive) called - yes, truly - George Stevenson.

With the advantage of hindsight, it would seem that fourteen months were too short a time for people to put in the notional 1000 hours of spare time needed to create a live steam loco; in the event, only nine Dyaks were ready, plus a multitude of cries of anguish from those whose entries were still unfinished. It had been considered that another three months would have quadrupled the number of entries. A second competition with Curly's own more modest prize, plus others from Percival Marshall & Co. and suppliers of castings and fittings took place the following year.

DYAK of 1934 was the 2½in gauge locomotive set for tyro builders competing to win George Stevenson's beautiful silver casket. The master built his own definitive edition, DYAK QUEEN, herewith illustrated.

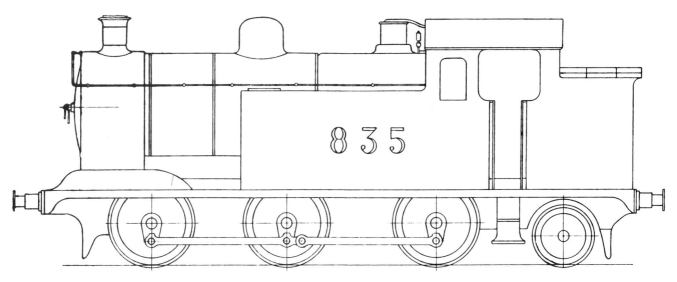

8.35 TO THE CITY was a gauge 1 version of Great Eastern No. 835, described in English Mechanics during 1934.

5.15 FROM THE CITY was also a gauge 1 daily-breaders' locomotive but Great Western this time, after the style of the '51XX' class.

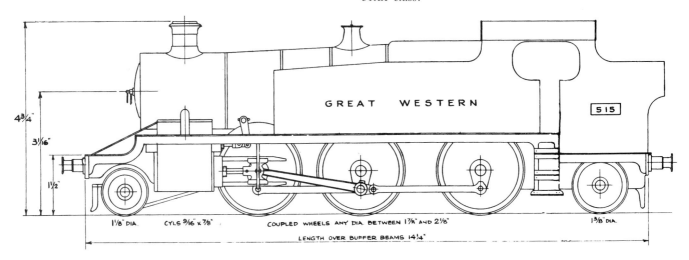

DAISY DRUMMOND and 'LBSCR' were two similar simple gauge 1 locomotives offered during 1934 to Model Engineer and English Mechanics readers respectively. The illustration depicts the L&SWR style of the former.

EVA MAY was Curly's first for 5in gauge; offered in both tank and tender versions for English Mechanics in 1933.

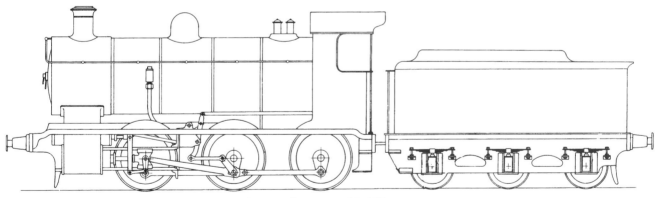

'EVA MAY' AS A TENDER ENGINE

The master built his own version called (modestly) *Dyak Queen*, to provide illustrations for this series; he did the same for *Purley Grange*, *Mary Ann* (LNER J39 class 0-6-0) *Maisie* and *Josie*. *Josie* was the only American locomotive design published during the period; she was an O gauge New York Central 4-6-4, remarkable in that she was coal-fired.

Amongst the other five locomotives built during this period was a pathfinding 4-6-2 of vaguely LMS aspect called *Fernanda*. *Fernanda* was the test vehicle for the piston-valve cylinders which were later to be offered for so many 'LBSC' locomotives.

The process of running locomotives which, after all, was the main object in building them, led to one of the most brilliant examples ever of 'LBSC's' light and now sure touch with serious instruction. This was a dissertation on engine-driving which appeared in March 1938; a fitting conclusion to a decade of triumph for him......

Driving and Firing

Bad workmen, it is said, always blame their tools. Maybe; but I know to two good amendments. The workman may not be bad, but only inexperienced or even ignorant. The tools themselves may be of good

MARY ANN was a neat representation in 2½in gauge of the LNER class 'J39'; it appeared in the Model Engineering during 1934. Curly's own edition is shown here; she turned up recently in the possession of George Williams.

design, but badly made, so that great skill is necessary to do good work with them. Both the saying, and the amendments, apply to the operation of a little locomotive. The finest engine ever put on rails will fail if not handled correctly, either from carelessness, ignorance, or indifference. A poor engine may be made to put up a passable show, by skilful handling; many a full-size engine-driver can tell a tale about that! But your humble servant invariably gets the blame if a 'live steam' engine, badly built by somebody who doesn't stick to instructions, but goes to work in a slipshod happy-go-lucky way, doesn't perform as expected! Such is the way of the world.

Builders write, now and again, to say their engines won't steam, or, maybe, maintain pressure for a short while, then suddenly lost it and will not pick up; go 'stony' when the pump or injector is put on, or need the blower going hard all the time when running; and a hundred-and-one other complaints. In ninety-nine cases out of a hundred, the only trouble is lack of skill in driving and firing. A 'live-steamer' such as 'Purley Grange', or the 'Southern Maid', or any other engine described in these notes, differs only from its big sister in point of size, and in the essential detail alterations necessitated by the fact that you can't 'scale' Nature - e.g., a few comparatively large boiler-tubes, instead of a couple of hundred tiny ones. Therefore, it needs the same treatment as the full-sized engine, to get the same standard of performance. Let's compare a run on big sister, with a trip on baby and you'll see for yourself.

Now we'll suppose you are going to drive the up restaurant-car express (nicknamed the 'Clinkemdoodle' by the railwaymen) leaving Biffington (Market Square) at 4.30p.m., and due in London (Padston Cross) at 6.30p.m. - eh? why, certainly the same day! - and as the

terminals are 135 miles apart, there won't be much time for sleep. Train is heavy steel rolling stock, nine bogies and two refreshement-cars, about 420 tons all told; your engine is 'Susan', a big 4-6-0, with 22ins. x 28in. cylinders, 6ft. 9ins. wheels, and a large well-proportioned Belpaire boiler with taper barrel. Your mate, Dick, is an artist with the shovel, and knows exactly what to do and when to do it. Now we're all set; 'Susan' is blowing off gently, humming like an excited animal; the signal shows green, the last doors are slammed, and Tim, the guard, waves his flag. 'Who-o-e-e!' remarks 'Susan', in response to a tug at the whistle cord, and you open the regulator. Now, gently does it, boy; don't give her too much, or the power behind those big pistons will make her dance and try to blow the smoke-boards through the station roof. More haste, less speed. That's it - she gives a truly feminine deep sigh and a little shiver - who says engines haven't life? - as she takes hold of the coaches, and then off we go. Whup! whup! whup! come the terrific exhaust cracks from the short fat chimney as 'Susan', rapidly accelerating, yanks the train from under the glass arch and noses through the maze of crossings. Now you notch up a little and pull the

HOLLYWOOD ANNIE was a suggestion for a Yankee version of Annie Boddie.

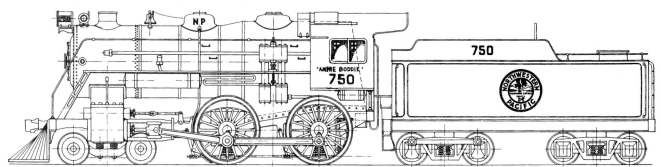

FERNANDA was an experimental pacific in LMS style, made to test the feasibility of adopting piston valves for 2½in gauge locomotives. She remained in Curly's possession until the end and is now owned by Jack Calderbank.

GREEN ARROW was a 2½in gauge version of the then new LNER 'V2' class, complete with 3 cylinders and Holcroft 2-to-1 valve gear. The design was serialised in English Mechanics.

regulator just over half open; the exhaust cracks ease up a little, but they are rapidly merging together. Dick is now busy with his shovel; he's also got his injector on. Faster and faster goes 'Susan' she knows, as well as you do, that she's no time to waste; *now* you see the value of those big cylinders; they maintain a high acceleration, and that's where you save the minutes, just like 'Miss Milly Amp's' outfits. Up pop the green colour-lights; whizz! through a suburban station; whoosh! under a low bridge. Now, laddie, fetch the lever back a shade more until you feel her 'kick', then ease it again until she just doesn't; pull the regulator wide open. 'Susie' is only purring now, but jiminy! isn't she moving! Sixty? Aye - *and the rest.*

When you've plenty of power, whether locomotive or human being, you always use it *judiciously,* if you know your job. For instance, Dicky, here, is a shining light in the depot football team, and can sling a two-cwt. sack of coal over his shoulder with one hand. But you saw, when we had that cup of tea together in the buffet that he lifted his cup to his lips quite gently; he didn't put the 'two-cwt heave' into it, so that the tea shot over his shoulder and half drowned that 'Miss Lipstick' who was just behind us. See what I mean? Just look at him now, firing, 'by the signals', he saw the distant was 'off' so he's popping a bit on, just here he wants it, because we won't be checked for the next mile or two in any case, and that steam-gauge needle has to stick around the 250 mark.

Tinkleford - 5.16, dead on time; now there's the seven-mile bank. Ease the lever just a shade as 'Susan' feels the pull, so that the speed is kept up as high as possible without distressing her; there's one place on the lever, at about 25 per cent cut-off, at which she combines a maximum of speed and power, and pulls as though she'd take the coaches over the top of Mount Everest.

CLINK-BANG COLLIE was originally an inferior commercial product, rebuilt by Curly in 1926 for a client-friend. She was a replica of one of the Great Central type 2-8-0s supplied in large numbers to the War Department during World War II. In 1935, as this photo shows, she came back to him for a new boiler. This was of standard Great Western pattern; strangely enough, the GWR never reboilered any of the 'ROD' 2-8-0s with taper boilers, but this model represents an interesting and likely might-have-been.

Ah! - that's got it; you sense that she has settled down to her pull, though still doing her mile a minute. Notice how Dicky is firing, putting more coal on just as the blast has pulled the last lot up to full incandesence, and she wants to blow off? And the 'live steam' injector gives her the extra water needed for the extra steam.

'Over the top and the best of luck!' Two miles slight fall, and then forty-odd almost level; now, 'Susan' show us how a lady can sprint. Back comes the lever again to just below kicking point, 'Susie' blows off gently, as though clearing her lungs, and then - well, hold your own breath! Seventy - eighty - ninety - a hundred - look at your watch, Ready? Go ..... through!

Thirty-two seconds, eh? Old 'Susan's' certainly going some, isn't she? Here's Catbury cutting, and there's a short tunnel at the end; put your hands over yours ears as we dive in, or you'll be deaf for the rest of the trip.

LMS 2537 was a 2½in gauge Stanier 2-6-4T described in English Mechanics during 1935.

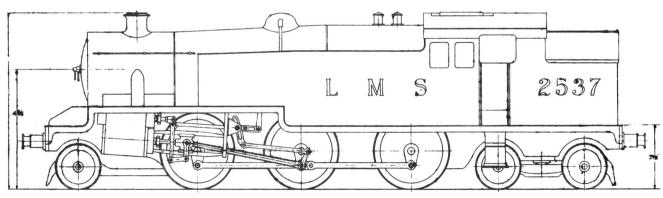

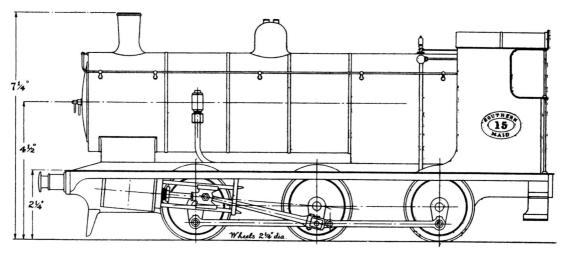

Dicky called 'off!' at the distant, but didn't fire? That's quite O.K., there's a service slack at Muggleton Jct., and we don't want to go through blowing off sky high. Open the blower a little, and shut the regulator; just a gentle brake application as we pass the goods yard - that's the ticket. Now, here old 'Susan's' lovely voice - 'Whoooeeee!'. Not a bit like Gracie of Rochdale, but by goom laad, tha knows she's coming'! My, what a crowd on the platform; must be market-day, but we can't stop to pick any of 'em up. No more slacks after this; bring the lever back to running position once more, and give her all the regulator. 'Susan' rapidly gets into her stride again as Dick gets busy with his shovel, and soon the fire is in full-speed running trim once more.

Oil? We don't bother about that, with a couple of decent mechanical lubricators to look after cylinders and axleboxes. Water in the tender? Dicky dropped and scoop back at the trough, just before we got to Tinkleford bank, and there are some more at Petalborough, just ahead, and Nickleferry. No, don't check her, our scoop will pick up at any speed. How do I think you're shaping? - fine! I see you've already got the 'feel' of the engine, and have tumbled to the trick of juggling the lever to maintain even speed; but old 'Susan's' taken a fancy to you, that's the truth of the matter, and is showing you what she can do. Carry on.....

Well, here are the merry old suburban back gardens; five miles to go, and seven minutes left. Dicky has finished firing, although there's still full pressure, but the water is falling in the glass. Shut off at Dogbridge, she'll coast the rest - that's the idea. Give 'em a toot before we scoot past the goods and carriage sidings, in case there's anybody crossing the main roads. Brake, laddie - steady, not too violent, some of the arabs in the tea-car are just draining their cups - now release, let her drift around the last curve into Padston Cross; here's the terminal, brake again to ten miles an hour, hold the handle - whoa! and here we are, safe and sound, three yards from the stop buffers, 6.30 dead. Glad you enjoyed the trip; you see how a big engine is driven and fired; now if you call around to my home one afternoon, I'll show you 'Susan's' little sister, which is worked exactly the same way.

Through the Other End of the Telescope

Well, here's baby 'Susan'; the image of her big sister, isn't she? Same noise, same kind of smell, same everything except size. We haven't any 135-mile trip to do with her, but she goes at a higher speed and pulls a bigger load in proportion to size; and a fifty-minute non-stop run around this little line, about 90 laps, would equal the trip from Biffington to Padston Cross. I've already told you how we get up steam on a baby 'Susie', using an auxiliary blower, and starting the fire with wood or charcoal, because she is too small for natural draught. You see the water is near the top of the gauge, and the fire has just burnt through. She is just under working pressure, 80-lb., and the blower is on a little. Sit well over on the flat car don't fidget about, and you'll ride quite safely; a cyclist rides on a narrower gauge; I'll bet you never thought of that. Don't forget that the handles on baby 'Susie's' footplate work the same as those on big 'Susan'; but that handle sticking through like a damper, works the by-pass cock, as the little engine feeds her boiler with a pump.

SOUTHERN MAID was a neat and delightful 2½in gauge L&SWR -style 0-6-0 for beginners. The instructions in the Model Engineer were particularly thorough.

Open the regulator very steady, until you feel her pull; then give her just a little more, but don't let her slip. Bad enginemanship causes more slipping than big cylinders. Now you have to do Dick's job as well. Don't notch up yet, but shut the blower-valve, and pop a bit on the fire whilst she is puffing hard, a shovelful each side, and one at the back. Open the regulator a little more, and she will gather speed; now you can notch up, as the blast has pulled the fire through. The water is dropping in the glass, but she is just going to blow off, so shut the by-pass and let the lot go into the boiler. This will hold the steam pressure down for a minute or two, but, as the water gets up near the top nut, open the by-pass a little and endeavour to keep the water at the level. The fire will now be fully incandescent, and she will blow off again as the feed is reduced; so open the door and pop on some more coal, same as before. Now you're all set to break the Biffington-London record on a small scale, if you feel like it!

Little 'Susie's' mechanical lubricator will take care of the oiling, and all you have to do is to judge how often to fire her, and keep her to a safe speed. As the moving parts of a tiny locomotive are very light, and have practically no inertia, they can turn their wheels at a greater number of revolutions per minute; and, unless you have a big load behind the tender, the regulator will never have to be opened fully at working pressure.

When the safety-valve begins to blow off again, open the door and take a look at the fire. If it is right up to the door, don't put any more on for a minute or so, as too large a fire is worse than one too small; the blast won't pull the air through it. Leave the door open a shade, to prevent excessive blowing off. But, before the fire has a chance to sink down, feed in more coal, just a little, and shut the door. The pressure will fall a few pounds, but will rise again just as rapidly, as the coal catches alight; and so long as you keep on firing her thus, little and often, she will keep going and never vary more than a few pounds in pressure, just like her big sister.

Maybe your own road is not continuous, but only a small straight 'up-and-down'. In that case, *learn to operate the regulator so that the engine doesn't slip when starting from each end,* and don't bother about firing 'on the run'. At the same time, observe the 'little and often' firing rule, and never overload the box, nor let the fire get so low that the blower has to be used to liven it up. More water is used on up-and-down running than on continuous running, so it is best to leave the by-pass closed, and only open it if the water disappears out of sight in the top nut, and the boiler begins to prime. The heavy blast, caused by the starting at each end, also sends up the fuel consumption, same as on a suburban tank engine, trotting around with a stop-at-all stations train. On the up-and-down track, the blower should be kept on a little all the time. Finally, never try to start an engine notched up, and never smack the regulator wide open, which only caused the engine to 'lose its feet'. Engines performing on club and exhibition tracks are often derided as being badly designed and over-cylindered, when, all the time, the whole fault lies with the arab who is mishandling the regulator and lever.

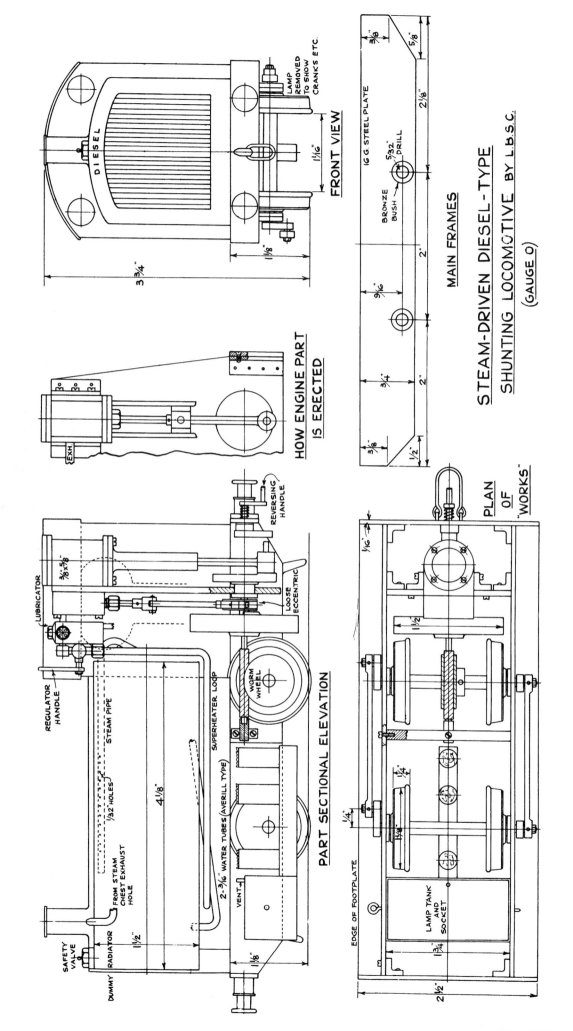

FRONT VIEW

LAMP REMOVED TO SHOW CRANKS ETC.

DIESEL

3¾"

1⅛"

1⅛"

MAIN FRAMES

STEAM-DRIVEN DIESEL-TYPE
SHUNTING LOCOMOTIVE BY L.B.S.C.
(GAUGE O)

16 G STEEL PLATE

BRONZE BUSH

5/32" DRILL

⅜"

⅝"

2⅛"

9/16"

2'

¾"

2'

⅜"

½"

HOW ENGINE PART IS ERECTED

3°

3°

EXH

REVERSING HANDLE

LUBRICATOR

REGULATOR HANDLE

SAFETY VALVE

DUMMY RADIATOR

FROM STEAM CHEST EXHAUST HOLE

1/32" HOLES

STEAM PIPE

⅜ × ⅝"

SUPERHEATER LOOP

LOOSE ECCENTRIC

WORM WHEEL

4⅛"

1½"

2 - 3/16" WATER TUBES (AVERILL TYPE)

VENT

1⅛"

PART SECTIONAL ELEVATION

PLAN OF "WORKS"

EDGE OF FOOTPLATE

LAMP TANK AND SOCKET

1½"

1/16"

1½"

¼"

¼"

1¼"

1¼"

1¾"

2½"

⅜"

44

UGLY DUCKLING, and another un-named but equally horrid abortion, were two diesel-outline steam-driven 'models' offered to readers of the Model Engineer and English Mechanics respectively in 1936. The later version is here shown.

GUARISANKA was a designer's sample of oil-fired DYAKETTE, the gauge 1 version of DYAK. Curly built it for a Mr. S. Y. Knight, alias 'Bro. Longhedge', who had a railway round his workshop with 4ft. 6in radius curves. On test she hauled her builder with ease.

PRINCESS ROYAL was a magnificent 2½in gauge version of the LMS Railway's first and then new Pacific, complete with 4 cylinders. She appeared in English Mechanics during 1932; a sketch adorned the Shops, Shed and Road articles in the rival journal for some years and this forms our illustration.

SHOPS, SHED AND ROAD

A Column of Live Steam

By "L.B.S.C."

Len Knight of North London SME drives his Helen Shorter *(a tender-engine version of* Helen Long*) on the Polar Route in 1952. The signal - an LB&SCR shunting signal - was actuated automatically by the trains; this plus a short length of track is being preserved as a memorial to Curly by Mavis Harriott.*

Chapter Eight

The scope of live steam notes widened considerably during the 1930s. For example, very little has so far been said about their contribution to small permanent way practice, but the 'Road' part of the Shops, Shed & Road was not neglected. Experiences riding on the superb Toonerville line in America had really sent Curly; he was taken over completely by the idea of a line on which continuous running was possible, although at the same time persuaded that a raised track was essential. Even so, for several years more, he had to be content with an 'up-and-downer'; indeed a cri-de-coeur in the M.E. asked if anyone within reasonable reach of Purley could offer testing facilities on a continuous line, with apparently no result.

Curly's new house lay alongside the Southern Railway main line just south of Purley Oaks Station. The first idea was to build a long straight line on a strip of land just inside the railway fence. This area was to be rented from the Southern but it turned out that the leopard had plenty of spots even in those days for the idea got strangled in the kind of red tape for which British Railways is presently famous. As one might expect the S.R. received a terrible roasting from Curly in his column for their creaky administration;

although this writer knows from first-hand that railways have every reason to be cautious with individuals who have peculiar requests concerned with their boundaries.

There was in fact a tongue of land between the gardens of the houses and the railway fence. Its owner was a property developer who found that the site was too narrow for another street of houses and so in the end let it go to the owner of No. 121. On this little plot Curly was able to erect the famous oblong POL (A) R route - short for Purley Oaks Light Railway - as well as a garage for his Morris car. The line was fully described in the Model Engineer towards the end of 1936.

Pre-cast concrete posts were set in the ground at 5ft. centres; then pressure-creosoted longitudinals were mounted on rebates cast into the posts. Sleepers of 'Bill Massive' size were nailed to these longitudinals and three (later four) brass rails were laid, providing for 1¾in., 2½in., and 3½in. gauge locomotives. The local full-size permanent way gang helped with the heavy work of erection. The total cost allowing for the new cost of material which was

The Polar Route - all of it. The locomotive is Ayesha.

recovered from the old track was as follows ......

	£.	s.	d.
50 concrete posts	8	2	6
420ft. of 4in. x 2in.)			
1300 sleepers)	5	18	9
all pressure creosoted)			
Bolts, washers, nails	14	-	
Brass Rails	9	0	0
Brass screws and washers for fixing rails.	2	9	-
Permanent way gang help	6	-	-
Woodworkers' assistance	7	4	-
	£39	8	3

The line measured 250ft. right round; the south curve, which was of 17ft. 6in. radius, could accommodate all but the largest 3½in. gauge locomotives. The north curve tracks are nowadays common in all English-speaking countries; for them all the main inspiration was this little race-track beside the London to Brighton main line.

Even so, the Polar Route was not the first British continuous raised passenger-carrying live steam road; this honour goes to the track of the Romford Model Engineering Club, whose 420ft. circuit was opened in 1934. A lap in 28 seconds on this line was reported by Curly to readers on 8th August 1935; the equivalent scale speed was 230 mph!

The most elaborate of the pre-war lines was the so-called giant racer at Burseldon, Hampshire, constructed by a man called Noel van Raalte, with whom Curly carried on a non-stop correspondence. A simple circuit of moderated length had been extended by building in a fly-over line and connecting in a second circuit. The gradient up to the fly-over was 1 in 70 and the sharpest curve 30ft. radius. It was magnificently laid out and equipped, Curly having been consulted on all the details. Van Raalte was prepared to entertain anyone who wanted to bring a locomotive for trial, and many did, especially members of the local (Southampton) club.

On Curly's first visit, he was trying out the 4-12-2 *Caterpillar*. As he passed over the summit flyover, he leant forward to close the regulator; at this moment the riding car derailed and brought the locomotive and Curly down with it. He described the event as 'taking part in one of the finest imitations of a full-size railroad wreck that I've ever experienced. The kind of thing you might see on the films, where the whole train plunges into the ravine, and the hero is discovered uninjured, lifting the locomotive to see if the sixpence that dropped out of his pocket is underneath it ..! An onlooker - Mr. C. S. Leiston, then secretary of the Southampton club - found that Curly demonstrated a mastery of railroad esperanto (one of his own favourite terms for the language which is such balm to the soul when undertaking many tasks connected with railways) that had to be heard to be believed.

Curly never claimed omniscience in small locomotive matters and often featured other people's ideas - with full acknowledgement - in his column. One very original mind was that of Edward Adams, whose Falls Grove (Really) Light Railway was described on 14th September, 1939. Adam's architect's training made for a structure which was strong only where it had to be. Longitudinals for example, were 6in. deep by ⅛in. wide compared with the 4in. by 2in. of the Polar Route, representing nearly 40%

Tom Glazebrook with some trepidation takes his lovely 'Fayette' Victoria across the high trestle on Noel Van Raalte's giant racer live-steam track at Bursledon, Hants.

Noel Van Raalte himself at Bursledon with the 2-8-8-2 Mallet Annabel *and one of his de luxe passenger cars.*

saving on the cost of material. There were no foundations - 15in. x 5in. timber bases spread the load sufficiently for ordinary ground to bear. In spite of (or because of?) this apparently flimsy construction the F.G.L.R. stood up well to a direct hit by a bomb during the blitz. Many other ingenious Adams ideas were to instruct and delight readers over the years and were always gratefully accepted by their chronicler.

Others were more jealous of their ideas and there was some acrimonious correspondence with Henry Greenly who fiercely demanded a formal public apology, as well as a half-guinea fee for using an idea claimed as his own, of recessing coil springs into dummy leaf springs and also into buffer heads; this latter so that there would be no protruding spindle to foul the frames. Curly replied (in January 1936) by denying the claim on the grounds that another and defunct firm of locomotive builders had been using the same ideas 25 years before, but hardly poured oil on troubled waters by adding (with a rare split infinitive showing the strength of his emotion!) ...' To deliberately copy any of your drawings is just about the last thing on earth that I would ever dream of doing; and I suggest that you know it. Very truly yours, L. Lawrence'. By such petty exchanges (on both sides) the famous quarrel went on.

'L.B.S.C.' the locomotive engineer we know; Lawrence the historian is however new to us. The little-known bit of history in question was in fact an account of this firm called Carson who made some really excellent commercial locomotives in primeval pre LBSC times. Alas, although they made better locomotives than their neighbours, unlike the proverbial mousetrap-makers, sufficient of the world did not beat a path to their door to ensure their survival. The firm went bankrupt in 1915; the account appeared in the M.E. in 1938.

Workshop equipment had so far had a rather modest amount of attention, but a welcome novelty in a new and shiny Model Engineer of early 1939 was a description of Curly's own tiny but superbly equipped locomotive-building shop. Many people must have found the Ninth Commandment ('Thou shalt not covet ...') hard to keep on reading the account, just as Curly himself felt when contemplating Noel van Raalte's superb equipment at Burseldon, described on 20th October 1938.

PURLEY GRANGE was serialised in the Model Engineer, starting in 1937. LBSC's original (this writer's favourite among all his productions) is shown in the superb photgraph by stockbroker Cyril Grose, himself a builder of GWR 2½in gauge locos. The original GWR 'Granges' had 68xx running numbers, but this one is named and numbered after Curly's own hacienda (his expression) in Grange Road, Purley.

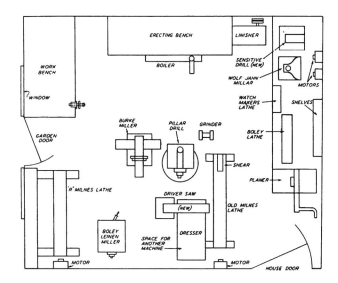

The compact layout of LBSCs workshop in the front room of No. 121 Grange Road as it was in 1939.

Illustrating Curly's thoughtfulness in caring for his flock, as well as being somewhere near the ultimate in model engineering instruction, came on 28th February 1935 when, under the heading 'LBSC - MD', our friend laid it on the line in describing ways for live-steamers to keep themselves in good shape, both for and while locomotive building. It is so full of wisdom that it should be offered in full ....

'it is funny - darned funny - how one thing leads to another. That chance observation about a visit to the dentist, and a couple of days 'under the weather' in consequence, not only brought some sympathetic notes hoping all was now O.K., but raised the question as to the effects of locomotive-building on the well-being of the arabs who indulge in it. Among points raised were, is it wise to tackle a brazing job when you have a cold; what exactly is the effect of the fumes of soldering fluid on the operator; and so on. Brothers suggested that by way of a little diversion and a useful one at that, we exchange the old greasy cap and 'slop' for a nurse's uniform, hang up the Red Cross outside the old lobby, and have five minutes' 'personal' discourse - in more than one sense! All serene - with pleasure, if it pleases you.

It will be a big surprise to followers of these notes to learn that your humble servant knows as much about human 'works' as those of a steam locomotive! It came about this way; being an inquisitive sort of merchant and realising, when in my 'teens that the human body is really a far more wonderful piece of mechanism than anything made of metal, thought I'd like to know the whys and wherefores. An old school mate, training for a teacher, was just about to take up a course in physiology at a training centre at the time; so I went with him to the classes, took both elementary and advanced courses, sat for examinations, and obtained first-class certificates. By the irony of fate, my friend failed. The knowledge gained has enabled me to keep free from illness, and

taught me how to counteract the effect of the permanent injury to my ankle due to a childhood accident; also now you know why I never need a muffler nor 'woollies'. Well, coming to the queries, there is not the slightest fear of locomotive-building operations having any dele ... (just a tick whilst I look at the dictionary) deleterious effects (gee-whiz!) on the operator, so long as simple precautions are taken. The actual brazing operation would not affect anybody with a cold; indeed, the gases from the coke might be slightly beneficial as they kill germs - colds were practically unknown among the enginemen in the old steam days on the London Undergound; but to stand over the job until dripping with perspiration, and then to go out in the damp and cold air to put the boiler in the pickle bath, is just asking for trouble. Even those in perfect health should if the weather is bad, wait a few minutes to cool off, and then put an old coat on; this simple precaution has saved many a dribbling nose! Some folk, however, can stand sudden changes of temperature and feel no ill effects at all.

As to the 'fumes' of soldering fluid, these are not exactly harmful, but they give rise to irritation of face and neck, if same are unprotected. The mischief comes in when the operator inadvertently scratches the skin with his dirty fingers. Being usually intent on the job, the scratch passes unnoticed, but, later, develops into a crop of blotches and pimples. Anybody who suffers from a tender skin should, before doing

A typical LBSC 'how-to-do-it' sketch of the way to rivet firebox crown-stays.

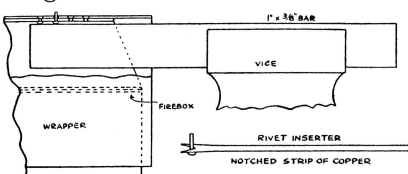

HOW TO RIVET CROWNSTAY FLANGES TO WRAPPER

PRINCESS MARINA was described in English Mechanics during 1935. She was a 3½in gauge replica of one of the Stanier 2-6-0s of the LMS railway.

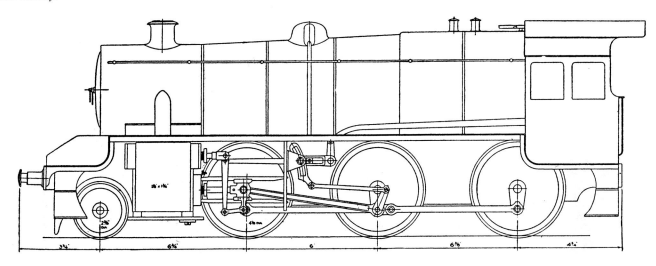

ANNABEL was a 2½in gauge U.S.-style Mallet locomotive reconditioned by Curly for Noel Van Raalte. Like TISHY, she came back to Purley after the latter's death, and is here seen in action on the Polar Route in charge of the late Tom Glazebrook, then 'lately returned from America. Note Yankee engineer's attire.

ALYS LOPER was an experimental 2½in gauge Great Western-style Mogul with outsize cylinders, ⅞in bore by 1⁵⁄₁₆in stroke; in spite of this, she had loose eccentric valve gear with fixed cut off. The trick was done by fixing the cut off at 40% and enabling the loco to start easily by providing nicks in the portface as starting ports.

TISHY, named after the famous cross-legged racehorse, was a 2½in gauge LNER 'Flying Scotsman' type Pacific. She was originally a dubious commercial product and Curly rebuilt and reboilered her for Noel Van Raalte ('Bro. Wholesale') of Bursledon. After his death she returned to Curly's possession as did the other Bursledon R.R. locos. Tishy is now owned by Mr. C. M. Moore, grandson of Cecil Moore who founded the Myford lathe firm.

LADY OF LYONESSE was a 2½in gauge version of a might-have-been, an enlarged Great Western 'Saint' with a 'King' boiler. She was built for a client-friend who was a lawyer, known as 'Bro. 6/8'.

S15 was a 2½in gauge design based on the Southern Railway class of that name, published in English Mechanics.

a lot of soldering, such as sweating up the stays on a boiler, wash his face and neck in hot water, and apply a little boric-acid ointment, or even vaseline. You can go right ahead then, and no 'fumes' will touch you; also you'll have a pleasant surprise next time you shave. Avoid inhaling the fumes as much as possible; but if you do happen to swallow a few mouthfuls which dries up your throat and makes you cough, take a drink of milk. It is the finest antidote for acid fumes that I know of, and I always drink a cupful after a heavy welding, brazing or sweating-up job - good news for our old friend the Minister of Agriculture! A very bad throat irritant is the 'smoke' which is given off by an overheated soldering-bit. Never get that into your lungs if you can possibly avoid it.

Most known brands of cutting oils are anti-septic, so there is no danger of poisoning an accidental cut or scratch from a lathe tool or metal chipping, by the soluble oil getting into it, as feared by one or two brothers. Working at speed, I get more than my fair share of damage to fingers, and gallons of Houghtlolard have not affected them in the slightest, except to wash away any dirt. Just recently I have been trying a British-refined cutting oil, Sternol Tapoyl (this will please the 'super-redhots'), which did not affect the healing up of a badly skinned knuckle. But don't use unknown makes; the proprietor of the munition shop once yielded to the wiles of an oil traveller, and we had a barrel of cheap stuff delivered. In two days or so, half the girls had rashes start to break out on their hands and arms; needless to say, the rest of the contents of the barrel 'accidentally' went down the drain. Cheap and nasty!

Just one more bit of honest advice before we take in the sign - don't overdo it. If you feel tired, knock off right away; don't wait to do just that other little bit, or the chances are that you'll do it all wrong, and lose interest. They say a change of work is the best rest; but if your daily work keeps you on your feet all day, and then you put in three or four hours more, partly standing at a bench and partly pedalling a lathe or other machine, it is akin to burning the candle at both ends, and don't forget *Nature always collects her debts*. A tired man or woman cannot

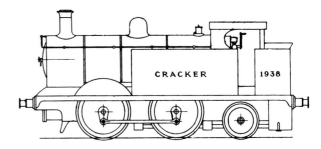

CRACKER was a simple locomotive for O gauge, described in English Mechanics.

do good work. Locomotive-building is work (incidentally, don't I know it!) even if done for pleasure; and work of any kind demands energy from the human machine. No energy, no results; you know what happens to old-fashioned radio sets when the batteries run down. In some cases, an evening's real 'hard graft' is of great benefit, as in the case of anybody who sits at an office desk all day. Pedalling a lathe and pushing a file exercises his body and rests his brain, cancelling out the effects of the office work; see what I mean? Use discretion; don't spoil your engine, nor lose interest in the job by trying to do too much of it at once, and with that remark we will close our little 'consultation', and resume our engineman's cap and slop. P.S. - Keep a first aid box in your workshop!

If all this were not enough, Curly found time to contribute (in this case it had to be anonymously) to a part-work called Railway Wonders of the World. His serious and crystal-clear articles describing how valve gears and other parts of the steam locomotive work showed that he could have shone just as well in the full-size locomotive world as he did in the small one, given the chance.

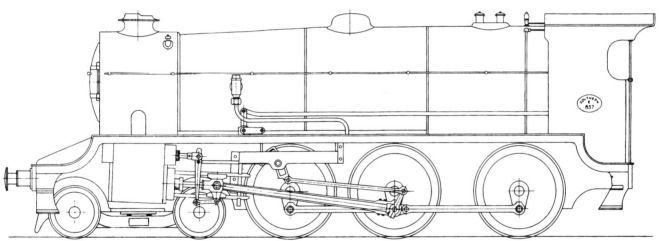

GENERAL ARRANGEMENT

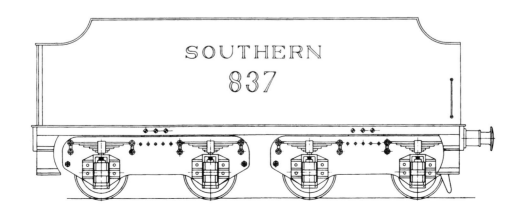

SOUTHERN
837

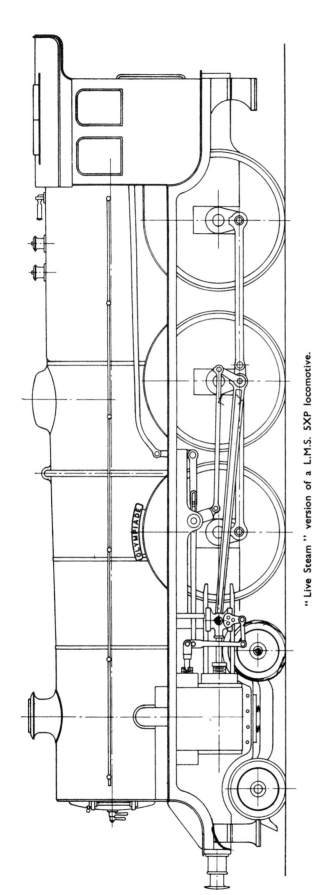

"Live Steam" version of a L.M.S. 5XP locomotive.

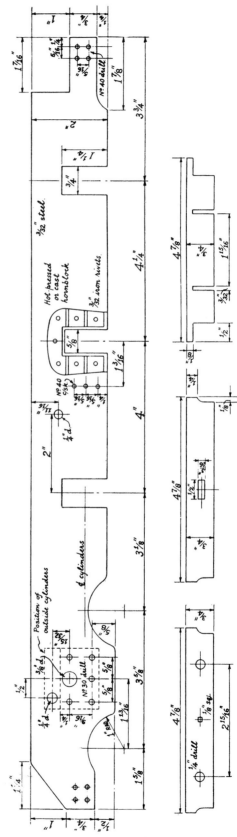

"Olympiade"—main frames, buffer and drag beams.

As we all know, the war-clouds began gathering over Europe in 1939, while at the same time a cloud 'as yet no bigger than a man's hand' had appeared over the horizon in Curly's small private world. His champion and mentor Percival Marshall ('our worthy Superintendent') had retired from editorship in favour of J. N. Maskelyne; while a man called Kenneth Garcke took over more and more the reins of managing the business, although Percival Marshall's name remained at the head of the list of Directors.

That new glossy Model Engineer appeared in January 1939 at it was an ominous sign that LBSC at first only contributed in alternate weeks. No doubt readers complained, for by May his contribution went back to being weekly again, although no longer called Shops, Shed & Road. It now appears that he was put under pressure to sign a less advantageous contract, as the following letter shows ...

PERCIVAL MARSHALL & CO. LTD.
13.16 Fisher Street, Southampton Row
LONDON.W.C.1   7th March, 1939

Dear Mr Lawrence,

   I said that upon my return from abroad I would draw up the terms of an agreement which you might consider accepting so that the future arrangements between yourself and Percival Marshall & Co. Ltd., should be quite clear and be placed on a proper basis and business footing.

          Percival Marshall & Co. Ltd., in consideration of:

1. Receiving from you an average of at least two pages of written matter, together with necessary illustrations and drawings, each week, to the requirements of the editor or any person acting upon the Editor's instruction, the matter to be used or not at the discretion of the Editor.
2. Regarding yourself as being retained entirely by Percival Marshall & Co. Ltd., for the purposes of your literary work and agreeing not to write in any circumstances under any title or pen name for any other publisher or Publishing House which may in any way be construed as being in competition with the Company without having received written permission to do so from Percival Marshall & Co. Ltd.

GEORGE THE FIFTH was originally a commercial job to a Henry Greenly design for 3¼in gauge. Curly rebuilt her, altering the gauge to 3½in., for Colonel Simpson, a noted LNWR enthusiast.

3. Percival Marshall & Co. Ltd., having the proprietary use of the pen name LBSC.
4. The copy-right of all matter written by yourself being vested in the Company.
5. You refraining from taking any action, verbal or otherwise which can in any way be construed to be harmful to the goodwill or 'The Model Engineer' and/or other publication produced by the Company.

will pay you £204. (two hundred and four pounds) per annum, payable monthly on or about the 15th of each month.

   If either party should fail to comply with the terms of this agreement then the other party may, without previous notice, regarding this agreement as immediately null and void. This agreement is for one year as from 1st April, 1939 and is there-after terminable by either party upon giving six months notice in writing. This agreement is to take the place of any other agreement, verbal or otherwise, which may at any time have been made between the parties.

   I shall be pleased to receive your comments, approval or otherwise, at your early convenience. You will note that I have suggested that this new arrangement should commence on 1st April 1939 but if this is too early I shall be pleased to consider any other legal points. You will bear in mind that the arrangement already entered into between yourself and Mr. Maskelyne will remain in force until the 30th June 1939, or such earlier date when that arrangement is superseded by this new agreement.

   I feel sure you will appreciate that the present arrangement was merely of a temporary nature and that the rate of remuneration paid to yourself is uneconomical as far as this Company is concerned. I, therefore, in compliance with the last paragraph of letter of 16th November 1938 written to you by the Editor of 'The Model Engineer' confirming the present arrangement, hereby give you notice that this Company proposes to end that arrangement after 30th June 1939.

                    Yours faithfully,

                    (signed) Kenneth Garcke
                    Managing Director

Most of this did not happen; a vivid account of how Curly saw what did was given by him in a letter to William Leggett of Montreal, (owner of The Toad, Swamp and Punk Hollow R R) dated 20th November, 1939 ....

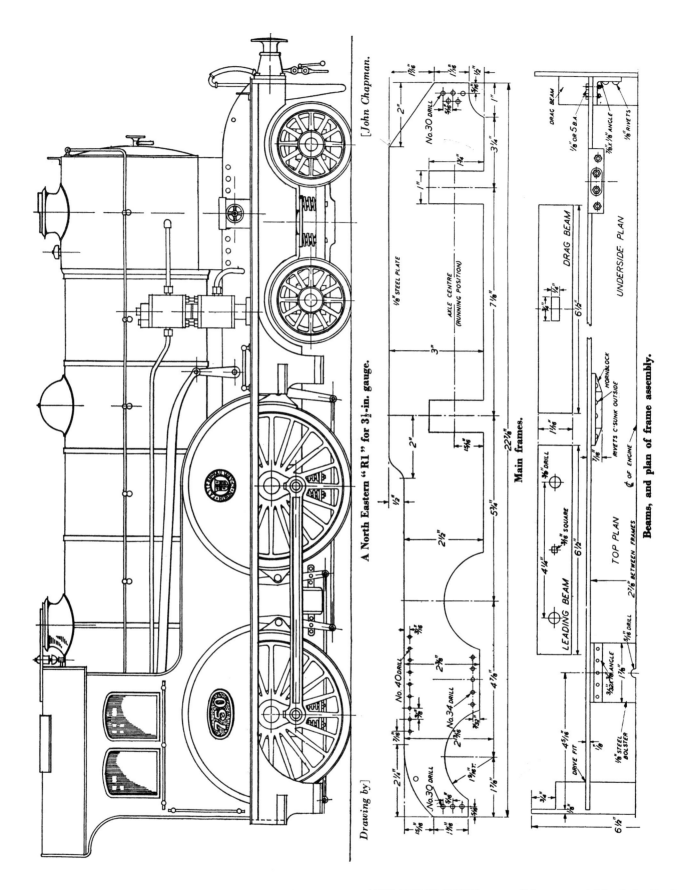

Drawing by]

A North Eastern "R1" for 3½-in. gauge.

[John Chapman.

Main frames.

Beams, and plan of frame assembly.

MISS TEN-TO-EIGHT was a 3½in gauge 4-4-0 of the North Eastern 'R' class, offered as a serial in the Model Engineer.

'In July 1938 the paper passed into the control of the parent company 'Electrical Press Ltd' and a new Editor was appointed, P.M. becoming just a figure-Ed. This bird was a pal of the old gang, and he at once started on my notes, censoring, pruning etc., so that my old style, lobby, characters, brotherhood, tea-bottle, etc. were soon eliminated. The old gang wanted to stage a comeback, so in the fall of that year the new sub-ed called on me and told me that after January 5th, 1939 I would not be needed every week, only alternate weeks, and technical stuff only was required. I was in the mood to quit right away and said so, but they offered me an increased rate to make up for the shortened copy, and I agreed to give it six months trial. I finished up the Olympiade series by the end of the year as requested, and supplied some wishywashy muck to follow, as per instructions.

When no LBSC appeared in the January 12th issue, the lid of L blew off. I had eighteen letters by the first post next morning wanting to know if I were ill, and was that the reason why Live Steam had gone wet of late. I told everybody the blunt truth. Letters poured in, and then they started on Fisher Street. Meetings were held at the clubs that had Live Steam sections, and resolutions were passed condemning the policy of the paper in changing its tone, trying to bring the old gang back again, raising the price and Lord knows what else. And the private letters that went in were a trifle overheated. Anyway, I got a letter from the Managing Director asking me to call and see him, which I did, and he promptly accused me of inspiring the opposition. I told him pretty straight that my trouble was to keep my followers in good order (old Greenly opened his trap a bit too wide at the last Ex. I attended and if it hadn't been for me his stand would have been wrecked and himself roughly-housed) and they didn't need any inspiration, I

told him about the letters I myself had received. Anyway he soon realised the truth and then gave the show away by offering me a contract for my exclusive services. I didn't see putting all my eggs in one basket and told him so; anyway, to cut a long story short, I agreed to carry on until the end of the six months on the existing agreement.

But something happened meanwhile. The lads of the village cancelled their subs for the week I wasn't in, so the circulation chart looked like the one over the bed in a fever hospital, and in a few weeks time I had an urgent S.O.S. to write every week again, reverting to the old style as near as I could, without making it slangy or too ungrammatical (they had to save their faces somehow!) So I did, and when the six months were up we had a new agreement whereby I reverted to my old page rate system of payment but at a slightly increased figure, and that is how things stand now.

The old gang evidently realised they weren't wanted anymore and the people who run the paper found out it didn't do to throw away dollars and cents for the sake of trying to boost them again, so that was that!

When the lid blew off Adolf's can they asked me to carry on as usual and if possible put in a little matter that might be of use to engineering dilutees on munitions etc., hence the reminiscences. Personally, I think Adolf's goose is cooked and that the little prayer which came to be the night of the great storm, went right to its destination and received attention. I'm not religious, as generally understood, but I have a childlike faith in Providence that needs neither outward show nor churchgoing, and it has never let me down yet.'

GWEN ELMS, whose name incorporated the initals of all the 'big four' railways, was an English Mechanics design for a 2½in gauge express locomotive with similarly mixed parentage.

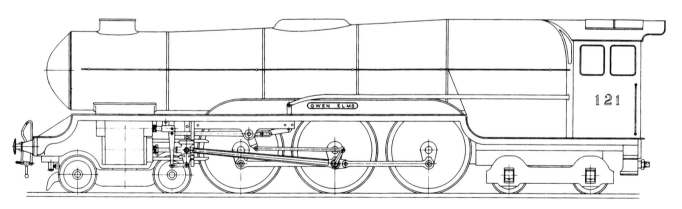

GENERAL ARRANGEMENT

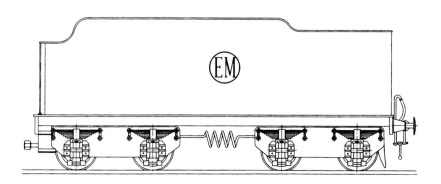

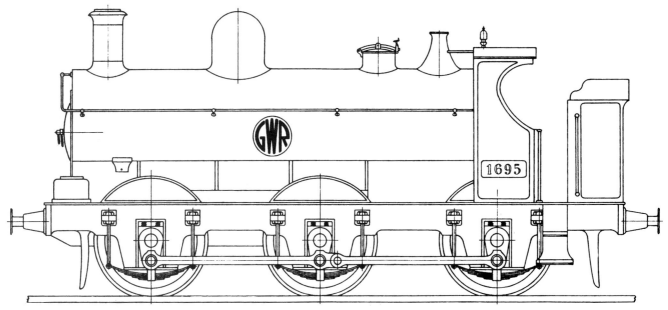

GWR 195 was a neat saddle-tank design for a 2½in gauge, appearing in english Mechanics.

In spite of all these troubles, perhaps this decade of the 1930s was Curly's greatest period; the able content and happy style of his notes appealed to a huge audience and his following increased accordingly. However, not quite all the Model Engineer's readers felt quite the same way. One was a Mr. O. G. Williams who wrote in to complain of 'Americanisms and lack of beautiful and dignified language'. Curly in his reply (29th July 1930) set out in typical fashion what was really the whole philosophy behind the racy columns of live steam ...

As for the 'beautiful and dignified language' part of the business - oh, gee! Now, friend Williams, I'm going to give you a hearty shake of the hand, in spirit, and bring to your notice what you will consider a bitter and unpleasant truth. Best part of the followers of the 'Live Steam' columns already know it; if they didn't they wouldn't be so numerous. It is just this. In England I had a very good friend. He had four legs and a tail, which latter component was usually in a state of violent oscillation when he was in good health. When it didn't oscillate, he needed a powder.

If I tried to put it, undisguised, in his mouth, he promptly spat it out again *ad infinitum*. If I cut open a soft cake, put the powder inside, and showed it to him, he immediately sat up on his hind-quarters and wouldn't get down again until he had demolished the lot with great relish. Now, friend Williams, I assure you and any other brother of like mind that if the 'Live Steam' was written in 'beautiful and dignified language' the good folk who would read it would be reduced to a minute fractional percentage of the huge crowd who have got no end of a kick out of my peculiar mixture of instruction and alleged amusement during the last six years. You see, brother, I'm just a human being - one of the crowd I'm writing for; we don't like powders, but they go down fine inside a cake! As to the railway slang, Americanisms, and so on and so forth, I was born and bred among locomotives, and I owe allegiance to both countries, my language is the only one I know, it amuses the 'Live Steam' fans, and it gets me where I want to go. 'Nuff sed!'

These last two words were perhaps the most famous of all the 'LBSC' phrases - one man even named his locomotive *Nuff Sed!*

OWL was an O gauge coal-fired 0-6-0 design with two inside cylinders, based on the LMS '4F' class. ►

DARLINGTON PLUS ALTOONA. Curly re-boilered and rebuilt this Atlantic for a client; the result was a cross between the North Eastern Railway and the Pennsylvania Railroad.

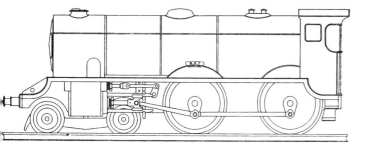

Chapter Nine

BAT was an 'O' gauge coal-fired 4-4-0 design.

So far as 'LBSC' was concerned the war meant business as usual. Both the magazines he wrote for became greatly contracted both in size and thickness, the actual amount of reading mattering falling by 75%, but the live steam notes continued unabated and undiminished. As regards the Model Engineer, in the first months a good deal of space was devoted to Curly's experience as manager of that aero-engine parts shop in world War I; the account given in Chapter 3 is based mainly on these notes. His first war-time projects were two O gauge locomotives; these were *Bat* and *Owl*, based respectively and rather loosely on the Southern Schools class 4-4-0, and the LMS 4F 0-6-0. The idea was that they could be run indoors in the blackout; hence the naming after creatures of the dark. Many *Bats* were built, but *Owl*, with 2 cylinders and two sets of Hackworth valve gears between the frames, was rather complicated for such a small machine and no example is known to have been completed.

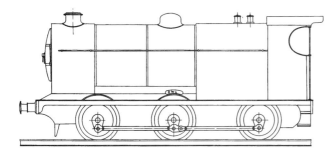

After the fall of France came the 'blitz' and the Lawrences lived in a part of Britain that got the name of 'bomb alley'. In Autumn 1940 the Model Engineer offices were destroyed but no issue was missed a hurried replacement saving the day for that of 10th October. The editorial department moved to the printers' works at Maidenhead. 121 Grange Road had a narrow escape when the next door house was gutted by incendiary bombs. In due time the German Air Force found occupation elsewhere but even so the issues of 1st and 8th May, 1941 did not appear 'due to enemy action'.

Despite all these distractions and although now around 60 years of age, Curly still found time to innovate. His *Rainhill* for 3½in. gauge, based on Stephenson's 'Rocket' type but 'modernised' has been built in its hundreds. Its simplicity made *Rainhill* ideal as the beginners' locomotive avoiding as it did - by being a representation of the most famous locomotive ever - the objection to most simple beginners' locomotives - viz; that they are replicas of industrial shunting engines, the least evocative ones of all. With *Ten-to-Eight* to cover Edwardian times and an archetypal Victorian express locomotive - the Great Eastern 2-4-0 *Petrolea* - described at great length (52 instalments second only to *Maisie's* 57) in 1943-1946, it only needed *Hielan' Lassie* and *GWR 1000* of 1946 to make up a complete history of the British express locomotive. The last-named was a rarity - an LBSC locomotive design without a name.

A notable innovation for readers was the words and music for piston-valve cylinders, used on 0-6-0T *P. V. Baker* (Patricia Violet Baker was one of Curly's munition girls) in 1943. Later they became standard. Suppliers have since reported a four-figure number of sales of castings and parts for little *Juliet*, a Hornby-like 0-4-0T on which many tyro locomotive builders cut their teeth. Generally speaking the 3½in. size of all the locomotives mentioned in the last two paragraphs dominated the decade as the *Appendix* shows, but other sizes were not forgotten. In April 1947, Curly entered the world of 5-inch gauge with two famous freight and passenger engines, 4-4-0 *Maid of Kent* and 0-6-0 *Minx* and they

COUNTY OF RUTLAND was Curly's own Bat; she had a GWR-style boiler and fittings.

JENNY LIND was the archetypal Stephenson standard 'Patentee' 2-2-2 of the early days of railways. This design for a 3½in gauge version appeared in English Mechanics.

The Purley Elevated line was a short 108ft line erected in 1942 for testing 5in gauge locomotives and others which found the curves of the Polar Route too sharp. AYESHA is shown on the main line, TISHY on the new one.

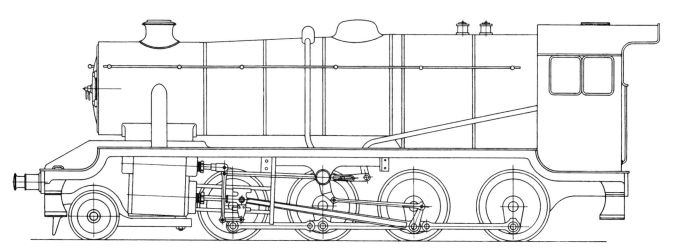

WD was an LMS Stanier 2-8-0 for 2½in gauge as adopted by the War Department to be the standard war-time locomotive. Curly described her in English Mechanics.

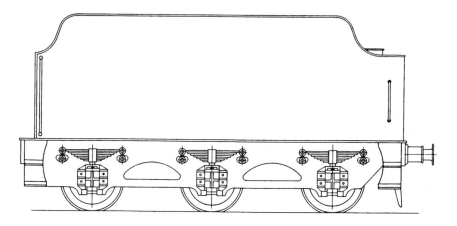

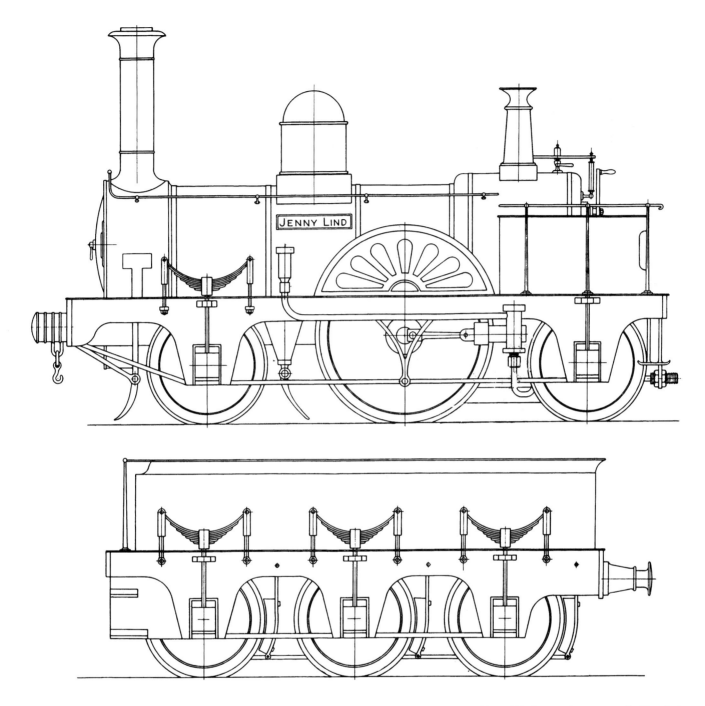

were to be the precursors of what was to become, 30 years later, the most popular size of live steamer. A new straight test track was erected at Purley, alongside the railway fence, because the 17ft. 6in. radius curves of the Polar Route were too sharp for most 5in. gauge engines and even a few 3½in. gauge ones.

During the bad years, readers who managed to see copies of the Model Engineer, but who were far from their home workshops, received some solace from Curly's reminiscences and tales of his early life. These appeared regularly and are the main source of material for the early chapters of this book. One thing stood out in all this - his up-bringing as a girl by a mother who gave him everything and a father who gave nothing. It is not surprising that a predilection for things feminine should arise out of such experience during his formative years.

Although no one could possibly know what went on in his mind at this distance in time, it does seem as though the war was when the feminine side of his nature began to assert itself and become dominant. Social contact was much reduced - even the M.E. editorial office was now out of the way in Berkshire - so there was less pressure on him to conform to the then rather more stereotyped ways of the outside world. Things like unisex dress were then far into the future; with no middle course available to him. Curly chose to indulge a preference for feminine ways and attire. Of course, since he was by now in his sixties, the ways he adopted were those of an old lady rather than a young woman. Yet there were so many things about his way of life that remained wholly unfeminine. For example, he was happily married to a wife of whom he invariably wrote with great affection - and certainly he

IRIS *the Antidote was Curly's reaction to the unusual Southern Railway Q1 class 0-6-0 which apeared the same year. His own version used a 2½in gauge* SOUTHERN MAID *chassis he had in stock, but the design in the Model Engineer was for 3½ gauge.*

LILA *was a beginners' design from English Mechanics.* ▶

CALEDONIAN 769 *was rebuilt from a Carson original for 'Bill Massive'. She is now in the possession of Geoffrey Cashmore.*

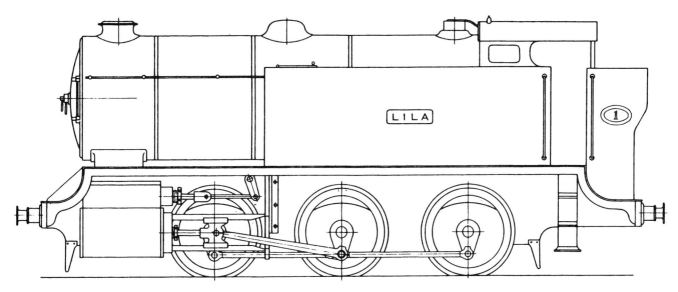

was not given to hiding his feelings when he had a pen in his hands! He retained great physical strength and of course the passion for locomotives and railways which drove him so hard was in itself the ultimate in non-feminine things. It may unequivocally be stated here that physically he remained wholly male to the end of this life.

In 1944 came the V1 flying bombs. Professor Jones in his recent book 'Most Secret War' describes how German agents in North London were 'turned' (in the jargon of the intelligence world) to report extra hits in that area, whereas those in South London were quietly put in the bag. So the Germans shortened their range-settings and accordingly a high proportion of the buzz-bombs fell short, in areas which were then not so heavily populated as Central London. Very neat, but a trifle hard on those who happened to live in places like leafy Purley. Incidentally, in the same pages there is mention of an occasion when a colleague's possession of a coal-fired gauge 1 steam locomotive got Professor Jones direct access to a certain Air Marshal, resulting in a change of procedure that saved many hundreds of British lives. It must certainly have been either an LBSC or an LBSC-influenced design.

Curly's response to this rain of high explosive from the skies was to become an evacuee. After a few nightmare days and nights he responded to an official suggestion that any one who could should leave the affected areas. Curly's Old Train Network came to the rescue and he was offered temporary accommodation on a farm near Stourbridge by a Mr. J. H. McDowell; Curly and 'Bro. Mac' enjoyed a wonderful Sunday out watching trains climbing the infamous 1 in 37 Lickey Incline.

After a week at Stourbridge, Curly and Mabel went on to stay with another client and chicken farmer called Smith. This was live steamer Bro. Coopie, who lived near Stafford. Here they stayed for six weeks. The live steam notes continued to appear without interruption and indeed their twentieth anniversary came about - with a celebratory article - whilst the author was an evacuee. Correspondence never let up; it is recorded that during Bank Holiday week there were 71 letters to answer.

Finally, a limited all-clear was sounded and on 8th September, 1944 the wanderers returned, to find No. 121 and its contents more or less intact. Neighbours had kept an eye on things. One nice thing; the Lawrences found a flood of offers of accommodation and hospitality from grateful readers. But because the live steam notes appeared five or six weeks after they were written, they were almost back home again when the articles describing the evacuation appeared on 31st August. Curly's thanks to Bro. Coopie

FIRS 245 was built as a present for Geoffrey Smith, the six-year old son of the chicken farmer who accommodated the Lawrences during the 'doodlebug' raids of 1944. He still has the engine.

Geoffrey and his sister Jean try out their new possession with a train of Millbro coaches on their father's 2½in gauge railway.

took the form of a present to the six-year-old son of the house. This was a spirit-fired 2½in. gauge LMS 4F 0-6-0 to run on the family scenic line known as the FIRS Railway. It was only the second nameless locomotive Curly built, but it went up to Stafford with no less love on that account.

Geoffrey Smith of Abingdon writes......

'I was the six-year-old for whom Curly built the '4F' in gratitude for facilities provided during his stay in Stafford. We still have it though we no longer have a 2½in. gauge track on which to run it.

My father had been acquainted with Curly for some years prior to 1944. Curly had rebuilt one of his engines, a Cardean, and they had corresponded on model engineering matters but had never met.

Curly arrived at our farm with very little warning in the summer of 1944. Although only six at the time, I vividly remember my first meeting with this strange creature who wore a long overcoat of late Victorian style (I'm told they were known as Ulster coats) above ladies' high-heeled shoes. His face was powdered and he carried a handbag. He invited me to come and talk to Aunty Curly! My father arranged for Curly and his 'good lady' to lodge with my grandmother, who occupied a semi-detached house on the main road at the bottom of our farm drive. The Lawrences stayed about two months which was plenty long enough to observe Curly at close quarters.

My father provided him with a workbench in one of his sheds and various other facilities. Nothing was ever right for him, as my father will gladly testify, but despite his prickly exterior he must have appreciated what was provided, otherwise we shouldn't have got the '4F'. Curly was very fond of children and possibly he found it easier to communicate with children than he did with adults. My father got along pretty well with him but there were some embarrassing scenes when others wanted to speak with him, even members of the model engineering fraternity with whom he had been in correspondence. The 4F was his own special way of saying thank you; something he seemed to find difficult to express in more direct terms.

We heard very little more of him after he returned to London. He was going to make us a Bantam Cock for which payment would have been made, but this never materialised.'

SYBIL the 'pre-Curly' was a rebuild of a 2½in gauge of a Carson L&NWR 'Precursor'.

MOLLY is still a favourite amoungst Curly's boxer designs; as described in the Model Engineer she was a close-to-prototype version of the LMS 'Jinty'.

RAINHILL for 3½in gauge, was based on Stephenson's 'Rocket', as altered after the famous trials. The design was published in the Model Engineer.

Talking of the output of the Purley Oaks locomotive shop, during these lean years it was a case not of quantity but of quality. But the quality was such as to make history.

Harold Holcroft, a senior locomotive engineer from the Southern Railway, was one of the world's leading experts on valve gear. He in fact designed the valve mechanism used extensively by Gresley (and usually known by that name) on the LNER, which enabled the valves of three cylinders to be worked by two sets of valve gear, in spite of the fact that their cranks were set at 120° to one another. Holcroft had now extended the principle to allow a four-cylinder locomotive, with cranks set at 45° in order to give eight beats to a turn, to have only two sets of valve gear.

Frustrated by unsuccessful attempts to have this gear applied to a full-size locomotive, Holcroft turned to Curly. The result was a Southern Railway might-have-been, a handsome 2½in. gauge 4-6-2 called *Tugboat Annie* and completed in 1942. The name was a dig at the then recent 'Merchant Navy' class on that line, of which

Curly greatly disapproved. *Tugboat Annie* is in excellent shape in the hands of Geoffrey Cashmore, who later became one of Curly's greatest friends and helped a lot with the writing of this book. A description of *Tugboat Annie* appeared in the professional press (Railway Gazette, 1942) and a how-to-do-it article on the valve gear in the Model Engineer.

One or two other people built locomotives which incorporated this highly ingenious valve gear. Mr. A. W. G. Tucker, a draughtsman from Beyer-Peacock of Manchester, made a superb 'Lord Nelson' class 4-6-0 fitted with it. This was fully described in the M.E. for 24th April 1947. All of this class, except one, had their four cranks set at 135° intervals and might well (but in fact did not) have had the Holcroft 4-to-2 gear. Tucker's *Lady Anna* was a magnificent model in 3½in. gauge with every detail all-present-and-correct; Curly was furious when she failed to win the Championship Cup at the 1947 Model Engineer Exhibition, on the sole grounds of having this modification to the prototype's valve gear.

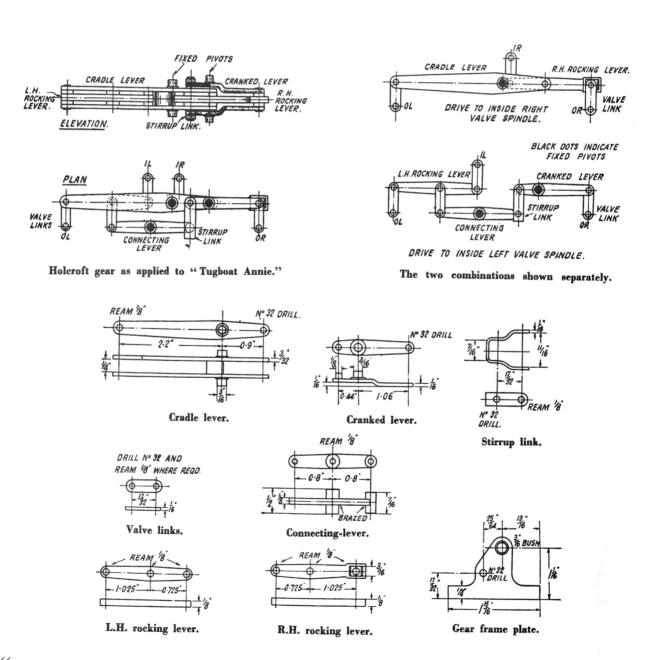

Holcroft gear as applied to "Tugboat Annie."

The two combinations shown separately.

Cradle lever.

Cranked lever.

Stirrup link.

Valve links.

Connecting-lever.

L.H. rocking lever.

R.H. rocking lever.

Gear frame plate.

TUGBOAT ANNIE was Curly's (and Harold Holcroft's) reply to Oliver Bulleid's 'Merchant Navy' class on the Southern Railway. She remained with Curly to the end and is now owned by Geoffrey Cashmore, whose grandson is seen driving in the action shot above. The lower picture shows the valve gear, of which the details are given opposite.

One thing that LBSC was always very cagey about in his notes was the time required to build a locomotive. However, Mr. Tucker provided a complete schedule of the hours he worked on *Lady Anna*. The times given below applied of course to a first-class craftsman and a perfectionist with an excellently equipped workshop making a fully detailed and very complex locomotive and they were no doubt a surprise to many people.

ENGINE:-

Part	*hours*
Frames	64
Hornblocks and stays	24½
Cylinders and covers	100
Piston valves and liners	29
Piston and rods	8
Valve-chest covers	26½
Valve spindles	13½
Cylinder drains	14½
Valve setting and adjustment	6
Guide bars and yokes	45½
Crossheads	32
Connecting-rods	44½
Coupling-rods	31
Driving wheels and axles	36½
Crank axle	17½
Coupled axleboxes	21
Crankpins and return cranks	10
Driving spring nuts & plates	7
Walschaerts gear	124
Holcroft gear	72
Reversing gear	23
Water pumps and driving gear	27
Oil pump and driving gear	34½
Vacuum pump	19½
Engine brake gear	56
Footplates and steps	78½
Footplate brackets	16
Driving wheel splashers	10
Bogies wheel splashers	3½
Buffers	15
Couplings	7
Drawbar details	5
Bolts and nuts	10
Nameplates	8
Cab	78
Boiler	70
Smokebox	37
Superheater	13
Regulator	15
Chimney and dome cover	14½
Lemaitre blastpipe	3
Firebars and ashpan	19
Boiler lagging & handrails	20½
Boiler fittings & mountings	102
Pipe work	53
Firehole doors	18½
Smoke deflectors	13½
Engine bogie	69
Erecting and assembly	60
Painting	71

Total hours on engine.......1697

TENDER:-

Part	*hours*
Tender frames	24
Footplating and steps	19½
Water tank	42
Hand Pump	18
Fittings	59½
Pipe work	12½
Bogie frames	54
Wheels and axles	16
Axleboxes	32½
Laminated springs	17
Brake gear	52½
Buffers	15
Couplings and sundries	7
Painting	18½

Total hours on tender......385

GRAND TOTAL......2082

If one devoted three hours on three nights a week and say five hours at each weekend to the job, it would take just three years.

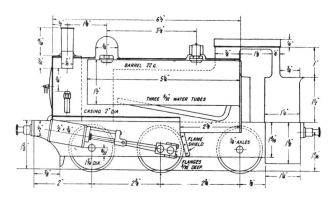

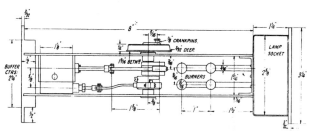

CHINGFORD EXPRESS was a gauge 1 'quickie' version of a Great Eastern 0-6-0T LNER class J69, the famous 'buck-jumpers'.

PRINCESS EVA was a JOSIE which Curly rebuilt and anglicised for a client in LMS style.

AUSTERE ADA was a design in 2½in. gauge from a replica of the 'Austerity' war-time locomotive. It was published in the Model Engineer.

PETROLEA was a very fully-described 3½in. gauge version of a Great Eastern 2-4-0. The series was the second longest running serial published in the Model Engineer.

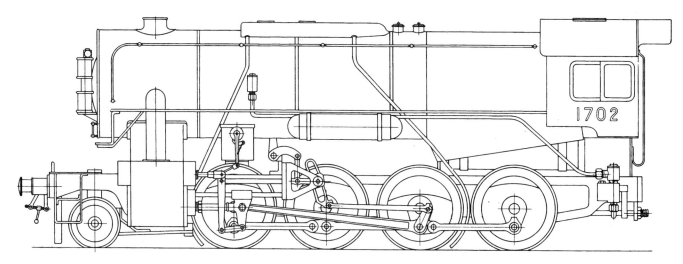

U. S. AUSTERITY was the American counterpart of ADA, as running on the full size railways of Britain in large numbers at that time; It was an English Mechanics design.

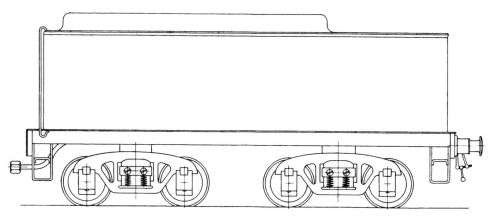

OLGA was a 3½in. gauge Carson 'Precursor Tank' of the LNWR, rebuilt with a coal-fired boiler by Curly and in his possession at the end. She is now owned by Geoffrey Cashmore.

JEANIE DEANS' controls and cab.

The famous Francis Webb had designed for the London & North Western Railway, of which he was Chief Mechanical Engineer, a series of compound locomotives. Alas, they tended to choke themselves when running and there were other idiosyncrasies such as the two driving axles revolving in opposite directions when the regulator was opened. Now Curly had often thought he knew what was wrong and that it was quite simple to put right. You see, Webb would never listen to any criticism - indeed, anyone who tried to tell him where was anything wrong would find it the last thing he ever did whilst in the pay of the LNWR. Anyway, the *Jeanie Deans*

of 1946 was just like her original of years before, but with one difference, a special intercepting valve to connect the low pressure steam chest with the exhaust pipe for use on starting. There was also a second superheater to reheat the steam between the high and low pressure cylinders. No how-to-do-it article on *Jeanie* ever appeared, but Roy Donaldson made a set of drawings (Curly had not needed to make any), copies of which were still available. A number of other successful *Jeanies* have been built but the original, which was later in the possession of railway tycoon Reggie Hanks, was stolen from his house at Oxford and has disappeared.

JEANIE DEANS was a replica of the LNWR Webb compound of that name. Curly's modifications overcame the sluggishness and other problems from which the prototype suffered. No construction serial was published but drawings were made available. Jeanie stayed with Curly; after he died she went to Reggie Hanks at Oxford from whose house she was stolen.

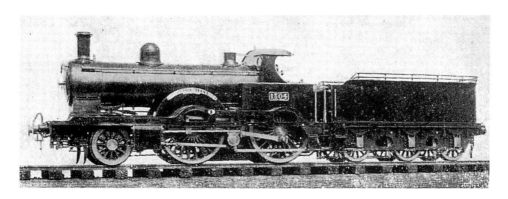

The Model Engineer relied very heavily on LBSC during the war; to some extent and in this respect the 1940s decade was like the early halcyon days of Shops, Shed and Road. This was a situation which was not to last, but, in the meantime, when admonition was needed it was set out in a dignified way as the following handwritten letter from a real gentleman shows......

Jan. 6th 1947

Dear Bro. Curly,

Thank you so much for your note. Don't worry too much about the shaking of the pepper-pot. Our blue pencil will see to that! I have heard a lot about it just lately - it is most regrettable, and I can only regard it as a form of insanity.

Your position in the hearts of your readers is much too secure to let such outbursts worry you unduly - remember Nelson's blind eye at Trafalgar, and follow suit.

I should be glad to raise a glass - a full one - to you at the next M. E. Exhibition, if you will be visible on that occasion. What about it?

Full speed ahead!

Yours as ever,

(signed) P.M.

The man referred to as 'pepper-pot' was a certain K. N. ('Cayenne') Harris, who was rather given to tart comments on LBSC and all his works, as well as a certain tendency to pull rank as a qualified mechanical engineer. Percival Marshall was tactfully pointing out to Curly that his equally tart rejoinders were better left unsaid.

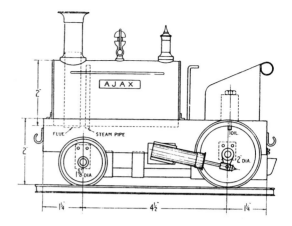

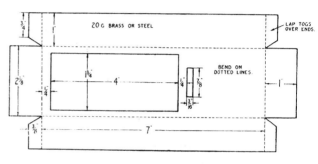

This version of AJAX, considerably superior to Curly's first locomotive was offered to Model Engineer readers in late 1947 as a Christmas toy for the children.

P. V. BAKER, named after Patricia Violet Baker, one of Curly's munition girls, was a 3½in gauge loco with piston-valve cylinders and Baker valve gear; she was described in the Model Engineer during 1945. Baker gear details shown below.

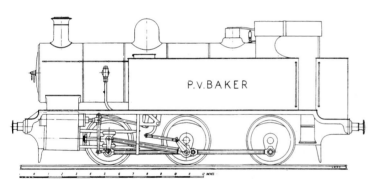

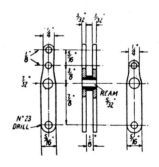

Reverse yoke.

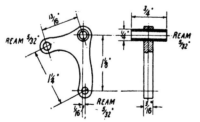

Bell crank.

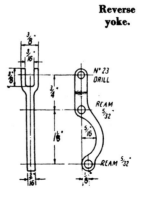

Gear connecting-rod.

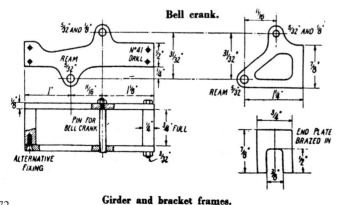

Girder and bracket frames.

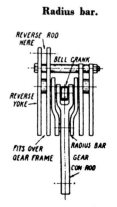

Radius bar.

End view of assembly.

CHARLES ROUS-MARTEN was a very old Atlantic type which anticipated (Curly called her 'The Anticipator') that GNR locomotive which was articulated to its tender. She is also credited with being the first 2½in gauge locomotive to haul an adult living passenger. She visited Purley Oaks for a major overhaul in 1941.

▼ LADY CHARLOTTE was a 'lass of the Old Brigade which received a rebuild at the Grange Road locomotive works.

▼ ANCIENT LIGHTS alias FLYING HORSE was a case of new wine in an old bottle being all right; another Curly rebuild of a commercial model. She was in his hands at his death.

BANTAM COCK (LNER class 'V4') was a 3½in gauge edition of
Sir Nigel Gresley's smaller version of his Green Arrow; the 'V4'
described in English Mechanics during 1945.

COCK O' THE NORTH was a rebuild of a poor commercial model
of the LNER class 'P2'. She remained in Curly's possession and is
now owned by Jack Calderbank.

The HIELAN' LASSIE design in the Model Engineer was based on the Thompson rebuild of the Gresley Pacific Great Northern. *She was offerd in 3½in gauge with piston or slide valves, Walschaerts or Baker valve gear.*

MOLLYETTE was a toy rather than a reduced O gauge version of MOLLY. This photograph shows Curly's own example.

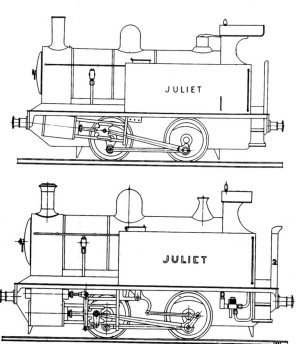

GWR 1000 was a 3½in gauge true-to-type model of what was later known as the 'Country' class; described in English Mechanics during 1946. Fred Stone built this one for the author.

JULIET was described in the Model Engineer during 1946. More Juliets were made than any other LBSC design. A later version (shown below) had Baker valve gear and cylinders with valves outside.

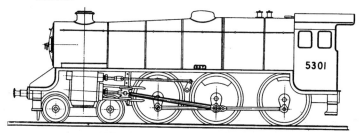

DOT was simplified gauge 1 version of DORRIS, whose description followed her mama in the Model Engineer in 1949.

DIANA was a coal-fired pacific version of DOT. In fact, a class 5 4-6-2 nearly appeared in the BR standard range, so making DIANA a nearly-was design.

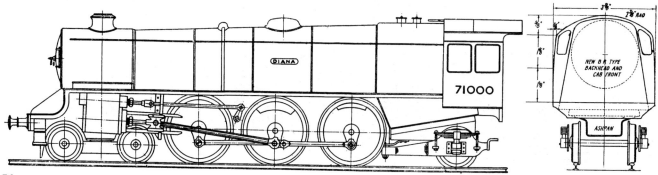

DORRIS, one of Curly's 'top ten', was a design for one of the legendary LMS Black Fives in 3½in gauge. This almost perfect example was made by Mr. Harrison of Boston and is owned by the author. He has numbered and named her 5428 'Eric Treacy' after his own full-size 'Black Five'. A close-up view of the motion is shown below.

In 1950 Curly was around the age of 70, when most men are enjoying retirement; for him this event was never to occur. The period began with his greatest scoop - *Britannia*. British Railways' then locomotive chief Robert Riddles was an LBSC fan and there had been correspondence between them regarding the details of the new express locomotives being built in secret for the newly nationalised railway system. The upshot was that a set of drawings was sent across to Purley, so that on 1st February 1951, the very day that big sister was unveiled at Marylebone for the press, the Model Engineer carried the first instalment of comprehensive words-and-music for a little one. A grateful Model Engineer awarded double pay for this serial as well they might for a great many small Britannias were and indeed are being built.

A very remarkable achievement was the five designs for different sizes of a North Eastern class TA 0-8-0 called *Netta*; in 1954-55 this mighty hauler was offered as a set of quins in all the gauges, the instructions running simultaneously. Ancient locomotive history was continued in the form of Canterbury & Whitstable Railway *Invicta* and Liverpool & Manchester Railway *Lion* (called *Canterbury Lamb* and *Titfield Thunderbolt* respectively in the M.E.) Both were offered as twin designs for 3½in. and 5in. gauges. An American Standard 4-4-0 called *Virginia* was another very popular and simple design, whilst Curly's G.W.R. pannier tank *Pansy* of 1958 for 5in. gauge caught him at his best with something for more advanced workers. The end of the *Pansy* notes on 19th March 1959 (a boiler and some details for a 3½in. gauge version appeared a few weeks later) was also the end of an era, for it was the last completed

LBSC serial that was to appear in the Model Engineer, or, indeed, anywhere. His last serial for Mechanics (a B.R. standard class 4-6-0) had appeared a few years earlier and he had also written for a short-lived publication called the Model Maker.

Particularly enchanting (and a feature of this period) were steam toys for the children; instructions for these would appear in time for them to be made for Christmas. They complemented two earlier toy steam locos, 0-6-0 *Mollyette* (1942) and 2-2-0 *Ajax* (1947). In 1950 there was a steam engine and in 1952 ((pity the neighbours) a steam calliope. 1953 and 1954 brought a steam crane and fire engine respectively, while the 1955 offering was a Stanley steam car 'Stanleyette'. This latter was more elaborate, needing three instalments to describe, but the first appeared earlier, giving the necessary additional time for construction. The last toy offered (1956) was a little steam hammer.

One cannot avoid criticising some of the other locomotive designs which appeared during the last decade. Some were unsuccessful and hence forgotten dishes from the past, reheated and served up again. They were still not very popular at the second time of asking. Narrow gauge *Zoe* of 1958 was very close to *Little Jack Horner* of 27 years earlier, while *Myrtle* and *Economette*, *Pixie* and *Nippy* had a similar kinship. *Ivy Hall* of 1955 was a really dreadful caricature of a G.W.R. Hall class; alleged to be a

BRITANNIA was a 3½in gauge replica of British Railways' class '7' 4-6-2. Letting off steam in the foreground is Curly's magnificent LB&SCR Grosvenor.

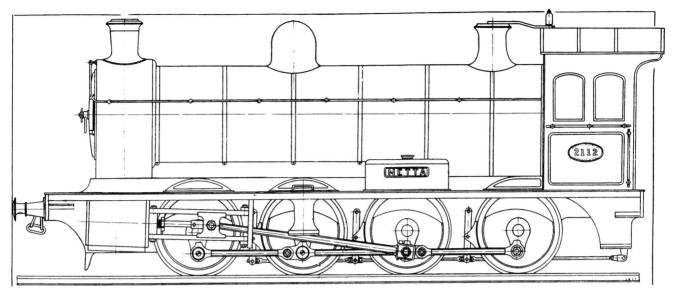

modernised version, it is understood that the design was done at the instigation of Mr. L. B. Howard, the then Editor. At the same time and as a riposte, Curly offered A. J. Reeves & Co., of Birmingham a real 'Hall' class. This was *Lickham Hall* of which many were and are being

built whilst no Ivy Halls are known to have seen the light of day. This was one of the incidents that in the end led to Curly's resignation.

In fact, Curly's resignation as a contributor to the Model Engineer was a long-drawn-out, messy and unpleasant affair. It was very much a case of 'a Pharaoh arose who knew not Joseph'. When J. N. Maskelyne ceased to be Editor Kenneth Garcke began introducing a number of people to the journal who were journalists

The NETTA designs were replicas of the legendary North Eastern 'T' class 0-8-0s. Curly ran simultaneous instructions for building NETTAs in five gauges (1¼, 1¾, 2½, 3½ and 5in), an incredible tour-de-force for a man then well over the proverbial three score and ten.

first and model engineers second; up until this time the senior staff had tended towards the reverse. Curly, of course, had been used to having a very free hand not only regarding the style of his contributions but also regarding their content. Now, not only was the style of his work heavily edited in a way he did not like, but also their content was dictated to him. His bitter protestations were regarded as wholly out of line with the Fleet Street traditions of 'conform or get out'.

A memo from Garcke to the then managing editor L.J. Waller, which was passed on to Curly, reads as follows:

> As you know, I am about to leave the office for the Continent and will be away for the next few days. I am therefore sorry that I shall be unable to discuss the following matter with you until my return.
>
> I have just noticed that LBSC is writing for 'Model Maker'. He is,

VERA, GERT and DAISY were similar simple beginners' designs produced specially for John Reeves' firm A. J. Reeves & Co. of Birmingham. Gert is now sold as REEVES.

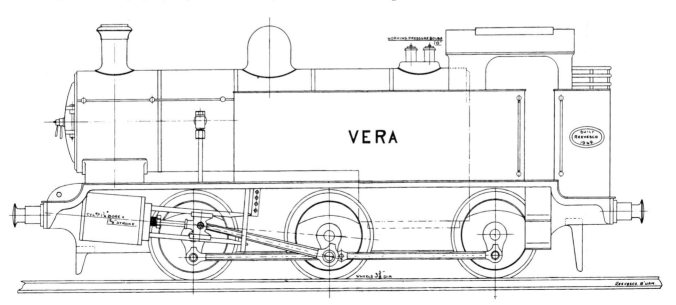

The "Canterbury Lamb"
in 3½-in. Gauge
by "L.B.S.C."

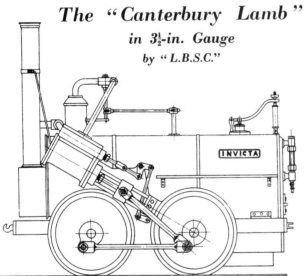

TITFIELD THUNDERBOLT was based on the star of the film of that name, to wit, the locomotive LION of the Liverpool & Manchester Railway. She was offered for both 3½in and 5in gauge in the Model Engineer during 1953. This example was built and runs in Holland. Curly's design followed the original in having 'gab' valve gear, the unhandy predecessor of link motion.

CANTERBURY LAMB was offered simultaneously for 3½in and 5in gauge. She was a replica of the Canterbury & Whitstable Railways INVICTA of 1830.

MONA was a simple 3½in gauge 0-6-2T with Hackworth valve gear offered to readers of the Model Maker. Curly's own example stayed with him and is now in the possession of Peter Roake.

of course, legally entitled to do so, but I regard such action by him to be unethical, especially in view of the very long connection he has had with the 'Model Engineer' and also in view of the recent correspondence I have had with him.

I presume that LBSC did not approach you prior to taking this action?

If I had had the time before my departure I would have written to him telling him that the 'Model Engineer' would refuse to accept any more contributions from him.

I propose to take this action on my return unless you can put up a very strong case for doing otherwise. So far as I am concerned you are at liberty to warn LBSC what action I am proposing to take.

Such ways were quite normal in the newspaper world and, indeed, efforts were being made to bring on fresh locomotive contributions as Curly's successors. Other people had managed to squeeze in the past; J. N. Maskelyne himself had offered a design for a G.W.R. outside-framed Armstrong Goods 0-6-0 for 5in. gauge in 1939, but this was before Curly had laid any claim to that size. After the war J. A. Austen-Walton ('Bro. Hyphen') offered his *Twin-Sisters* design for plain and detailed versions respectively of an L.M.S. 0-6-0T docks shunter; his problem seemed to be the same as Henry Greenly's forty years before, viz., that wide interests precluded the single-minded concentration needed to produce a regular weekly serial on locomotive building.

Curly's diaries from 1943 onwards have survived and these give a very detailed picture of his life; we know when he changed the washers on particular taps, exactly who called at his house or wrote. The overall picture is that of the life of a recluse who devoted himself absolutely to his self-appointed tasks. Casual callers are noted ... '.. but failed to get in'. The sight of someone looking over the fence was quite enough for him to bring a locomotive which was about to be run back into the house. It has

been several times mentioned that Curly spent sixteen hours a day six days a week on his work; readers might wonder why it wasn't seven. The reason is that the seventh day (not Sunday, that was the day for beginning another week's article) was devoted to Mabel; so we find Curly taking his own advice, for amongst the many hats he wore while writing his notes was one not previously mentioned called Marriage Guidance Counsellor!

Readers will appreciate that such dedication, coupled with the brilliance of which we are so well aware is a very unusual combination and very hard to replace. So, in searching for a substitute (and remember that Curly was at this time nearer 80 than 70), those who then ran the Model Engineer had problems. However, a certain Martin Evans proved to be equally dedicated and competent. No flamboyant genius, Evans' painstaking work and simple style suited many people; at the time of writing, nearly 30 years later, castings and parts for some 27 of his designs are on offer. Curly was by no means friendly to Martin Evans ('Copy-cat' Evans was about the nicest epithet used) and it is greatly to the latter's credit that over the years his great predecessor's work was always referred to with appreciation and admiration.

So, as far as LBSC was concerned, the heat was on; it does appear from correspondence which has survived that the then management were determined that he should do it their way or

BETTY was a might-have-been, a Southern Railway 2-6-2. A 3½in gauge edition was described in Model Maker. Curly's own example (here illustrated) is now owned by Eric Edney. The driver is Tom Luxford and on the far left is policeman Fred Harriott, once Curly's neighbour in Purley.

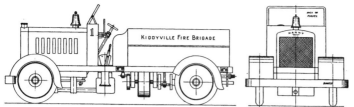

Curly's toys for the children were a feature of this period. Illustrated is his Steam Fire Engine described for Christmas 1954.

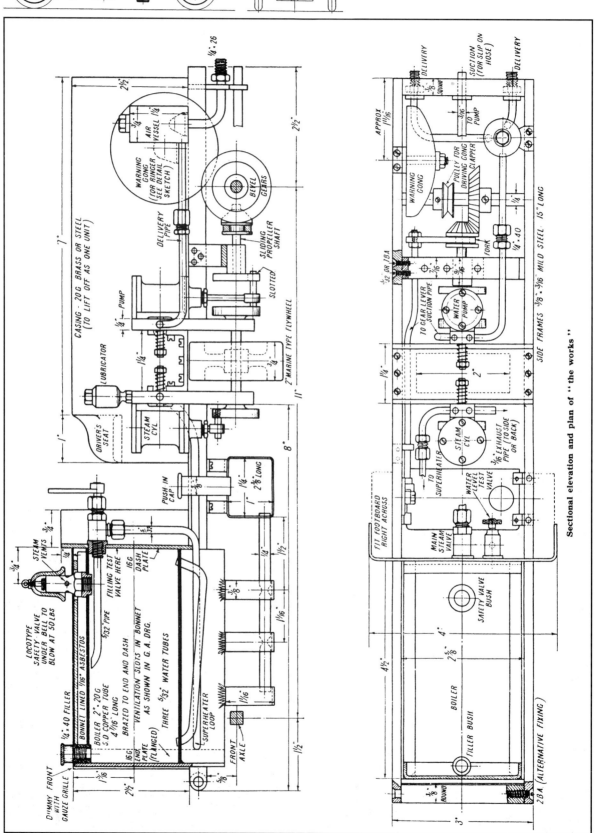

Sectional elevation and plan of "the works"

resign. A little while later he had come to the end of the road when, on 25th April 1959, he wrote to the Model Engineer in the following terms ...

121 Grange Road,
Purley Oaks, Surrey
April 25th. 1959.

D.J.Carter Esq.
19/20. Noel St.,
London, W.1.

Dear Mr. Carter,

I understand that you are now General Manager and in control of the 'Model Engineer', and it is with regret that, after over 34½ years of doing my best to serve the readers, I am tendering you my resignation. It is the result of trouble between the assistant editor, Mr. L. B. Howard, and myself. Would you please carefully consider the facts below.

I don't mind arguing with anyone about locomotive matters, but I cannot stand personal attacks at any price. Therefore when Mr. Howard published in the issue of Feb. 26th last, a letter from W.Donelly of South Africa containing statements that I was living on my reputation in a dreamland of old-time engines, and insinuating that I was in a state of senile decay, I was naturally annoyed, but had no wish to quibble about it in the Postbag columns.

Actions speak louder than words. To show that I was still very much alive and kicking, I made a drawing of an ultra-modern steam locomotive which would show any diesel how to do it, got out the first instalment of how to build a small edition and sent it in. Mr. Howard telephoned me and started quibbling about it, saying they couldn't publish it, etc. so I said 'all right, send it back'. However, later on he rang again, saying that it would be published, but only in six instalments.

In due course I sent the second instalment, prefixing it with a few words to the effect that as I was only allowed six instalments, I would have to omit description of certain components, variations, and tender. I enclosed a covering note that I did this as I wasn't going to take the blame for giving the customers short measure. Nothing wrong with that, surely, but it upset Mr. Howard, who wanted to put the onus on me. When I protested, he sent me two letters evidently written in a fit of ill-temper. He had previously requested me to do another old-time engine, and I agreed; I intended to do the two together, as I have done before, as it keeps more readers interested. Also the advertisers sell more supplies.

I still refused to take the blame for short measure, so the result was deadlock, and then came the episode which forced my decision to write no more.

In Feb. 19th issue there was an article on the subject of locomotive efficiency trials. In my article of April 9th issue I commented on this, as I had every right to do. On top of my full-size experience, I have been building little locomotives since I was a child of ten, and have here a small multiple-gauge railway automatically signalled, and eighteen steam locomotives of various types and sizes. I gave several reasons why a formula deciding the efficiency of any type or size of engine in a 15 min. run was impracticable. I also pointed out that so-called 'efficiency' trials were a source of jealousy and dissension in many cases, and gave a carefully-camouflaged account of an instance where

such a trial caused ill-feeling in a club, and broke up a long friendship between two members. I might add that I am a keen student of human nature, and all my life have faced up to facts as they exist.

This also upset Mr. Howard. I always understood that in journalism, it was the duty of the editor to be impartial as regards contributors. If he doesn't necessarily agree with what they write, he merely says so, and that is that. Contrary to this, Mr. Howard took advantage of his position to loose off a tirade against me in the 'Smoke Rings' column in the same issue. He as good as called me a damned liar about the story of jealousy and ill-feeling which I quoted; made other incorrect statements which betrayed a lack of locomotive knowledge, and finished by comparing a perfectly efficient locomotive which stalled on a grade on a damp and foggy evening because damp sand had choked the sandpipes, with a car which ran away on a hill owing to a faulty handbrake.

As this criticism was published, it gave me an unassailable right to have a reply published. A prisoner at the dock at the Old Bailey is entitled by law to state, either personally or by defending counsel, his reply to the charges made against him by the prosecution, so that the jury hears both sides of the case. I therefore wrote a reply to Mr. Howard's attack, but for the sake of the prestige of the magazine, I did it in more or less jocular form, in the well-known LBSC style which made my articles popular and so helped the circulation. Mr. Howard, apparently afraid of the verdict of the 'jury', otherwise the readers of the M.E., has refused to published it.

Now to publish an attack on a person, and then suppress a reasoned reply, is sheer tyranny. I will not tolerate Hitlerian dictation from any man breathing, so I am taking the only course left open, and can write no more while Mr. Howard is allowed to 'exercise the veto'. I might mention here, that I have received numerous complaints from readers of long standing, that my articles have lost their original attraction and sparkle. I have had to explain to them that it is no fault of mine, but a deliberate suppression of my original conversational way of writing. There is also considerable resentment at the way R.M. Evans has been put up to imitate the LBSC articles and drawings.

I regret if the above has bored you, but I felt that you should know the reason why I am resigning after such a long nonstop run. Will you please notify Mr. Garcke. I would have preferred to run the full course, and eventually finished in an atmosphere of friendliness and cordiality.

Trusting you are keeping well,

Very truly yours,

L. Lawrence

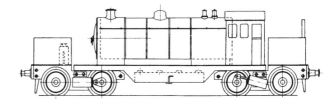

Brief descriptions of these two little O-gauge Beyer Garratts appeared in the Model Engineer in 1958.

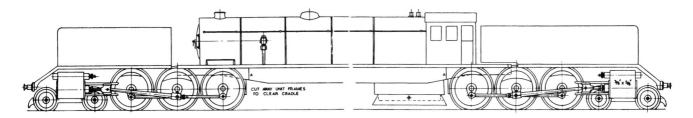

BR 75000 was the end of the road for 'L.B.S.C' in Mechanics, the last of some 30 designs Curly produced for that periodical and its predecessor English Mechanics. She was a standard BR class 4 4-6-0.

THE DUCHESS OF SWINDON design made a too brief appearance in the Model Engineer just before Curly resigned from the paper in June 1959. Some examples were built, including this one by Roy Coulcott who now lives in Canada. The tender is not yet finished.

LICKHAM HALL was a true GWR 'Hall' class design produced specially for A. J. Reeves & Co. of Birmingham. Not quite perfect, it shows the sort of result an inexperienced builder can achieve. Note the crosshead-driven waterpump where the prototype has a vacuum pump.

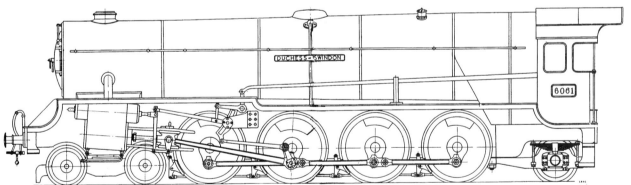

In this way the 34½ year non-stop run came to an end. The only issues missed were over Curly's sudden return from America in 1930 and the once-a-fortnight period in early 1939. Of course, the M.E. itself was briefly defeated by the General Strike of 1926, enemy action in 1941 and the energy crisis (coal this time!) of 1947. The date of the last article was 14th May; it contained a description of the frames and wheels for that ultra-modern steam locomotive, the magnificent *Duchess of Swindon*. One or two Duchesses were made, the builders being kept on the straight and narrow by correspondence. A rather unctuous and misleading appreciation (which Curly detested) appeared in the Model Engineer of 14th June 1959. So ended an era.

One of the deepest regrets that we must feel over the whole sad affair was this; during the first half of the decade Curly seemed to be working himself up to spilling the beans (his phrase) on a system of separate steam and exhaust valves for steam locomotives. When steam and exhaust is controlled by the same valve, however clever one is there has to be some compromise with what would ideally suit each function separately. Now each Christmas for some years a whole article has been devoted to a kind of locomotive fairytale set in the 1980s, with British Railways reverting to the old companies and of course to steam, but with 150 m p h plus speeds, as well as lady drivers. A 4-8-4 called *Queen Mabel* made a lot of running and suddenly in 1953 (30th July) there

PANSY was a very exact 5in gauge copy of one of the immortal GWR standard pannier tanks. She was Curly's last completed design, appearing in the Model Engineer in 1958.

"Cameras clicked and whired as 'Queen Mabel' backed on to the train"

popped out a serious article on Queen Mabel's valve gear - not a how-to-do-it one but a good description; you could call it the Baker-Holcroft-Lawrence gear. There are objections to poppet valves - although British Railways later claimed to have overcome most of them by the time they built 4-6-2 *Duke of Gloucester* - and so the arrangement provided for Baker valve gear to drive an

oscillating camshaft, on which there were cams which in turn drove conventional but separate piston valves for controlling steam admission and exhaust opening. Curly added 'Should it come to pass by virtue of circumstances, and the blessing of the K.B.P. (the Editor), that I describe how to build a little *Queen Mabel*, I shall then, all being well, give fully detailed drawings of the 'Thunder-and-Lightning' valve-gear, and once more put the cat amongst the pigeons ......'. This did not happen, although in 1955 there appeared '*Lillie* the Ideal Locomotive', a 4-6-2 which also had this arrangement of separate piston valves for steam and for exhaust, but this time there were only two cylinders 24in. bore by 18in. stroke! Alas, shortly after this the appearance of the *Ivy Hall* serial marked the beginning of the war of attrition, so the *Lillie* serial never came about either. Very tantalising!

Curly never made an experimental *Lillie* either, in spite of naming her after himself, but one locomotive that he did build at this time is worthy of mention. This was the LB&SCR single-wheeler *Grosvenor* which was finally completed - after a ten-year

LILLIE was a simpler version of Queen Mabel.

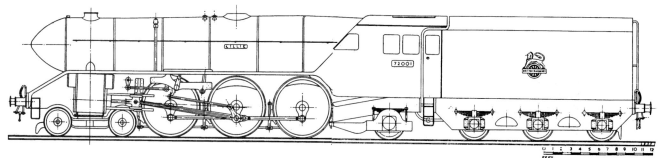

GROSVENOR the LB&SCR 2-2-2 in 3½in gauge was Curly's masterpiece and is a superb performer. She is now owned by Fred Harriot. The driver in this picture is David Chisnall.

construction period in 1957. The Purley Shops made a wonderful job of her, but inevitably there were some design changes, principally putting the valves on top of the cylinders instead of between them. Curly, who had become somewhat fey in his old age, explained how this came about....

I now come to the most curious experience I have ever had during a long lifetime of locomotive-building. Right from early childhood I have had vivid dreams. That isn't at all unusual, I grant you, but the outstanding feature of all mine is that they are all intensely realistic.

The original engine had the steam chest between the cylinders. Now on a 3½in. gauge job this means that the steam chest is going to be exceedingly cramped, and it would not accommodate the arrangement of ports and valves that I wanted to fit, beside being awkward for valve-setting. I pondered over this one evening, and looked up a book with details of the *Gladstone* cylinders and other parts of the Stroudley engines as a memory-refresher. In the book was a fine photographic reproduction of the immortal Billy himself, with a facsimile of his signature.

I was still thinking of these things when I went to bed and then came *the* dream. It is over eleven years ago now, and I can't recall the exact words of the conversation, but I'll relate as best I can. In the dream I was in my workshop again, and had the parts of the engine so far made on the bench when who should come in but Billy Stroudley himself!

With a cheery greeting he asked how I was getting on with the engine, and when I indicated the parts on the bench he picked up some of them and inspected them, holding them rather close to his eyes as he did so.

He then asked what I was going to do about the cylinders, referred to the small steam chest, and said that a better arrangement would be an advantage. I replied that I thought of using the *Gladstone* cylinders. He immediately said: 'You can't do that because the leading axle will come right in the way of the valve spindles.' I smiled and replied: 'Well, sir, it's your engine; what would you suggest if you were designing her now, with all the modern improvements?' He said: 'I'd turn the *Gladstone* cylinders upside down, and put the valves on top, drive through a rocking shaft, and use a long valve travel.'

I told him I was going to fit a superheater and a mechanical lubricator, and he nodded approval, adding, 'and don't forget an inspirator so that you can feed the boiler while she is standing still' - this with a chuckle.

After two or three more comments the dream faded out. Anyway it was so vivid that when I awoke in the morning I was not only able to remember it but I made some notes of what the old boy had said. I must confess to a cold shiver running down my back when I checked off and found that the front axle *actually did* cross the line of the valve spindles of a pair of *Gladstone* cylinders; that Billy *would* have held the blobs and gadgets close to his eyes when examining them as he was short-

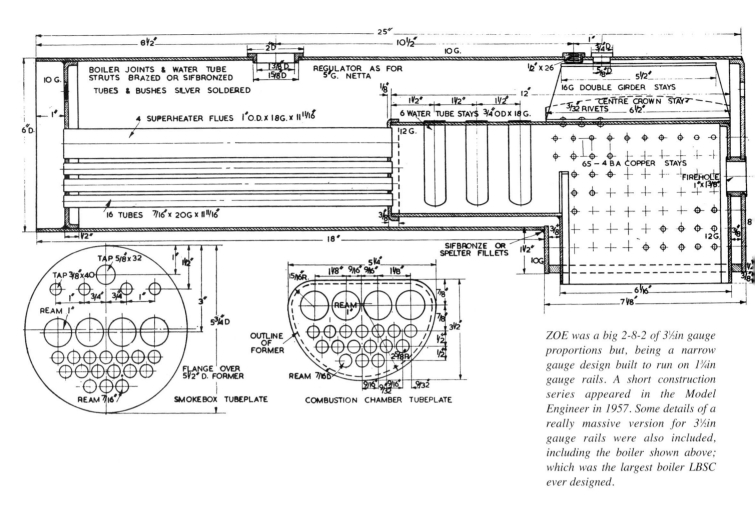

ZOE was a big 2-8-2 of 3½in gauge proportions but, being a narrow gauge design built to run on 1¾in gauge rails. A short construction series appeared in the Model Engineer in 1957. Some details of a really massive version for 3½in gauge rails were also included, including the boiler shown above; which was the largest boiler LBSC ever designed.

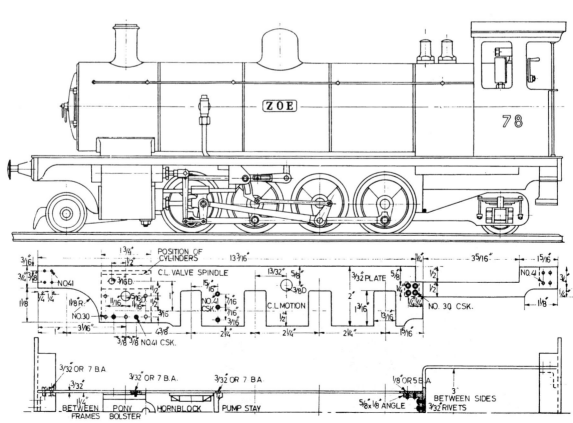

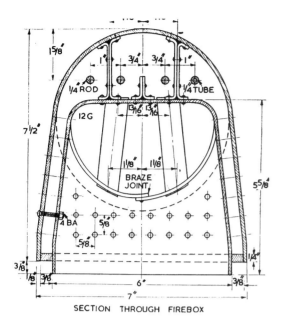

SECTION THROUGH FIREBOX

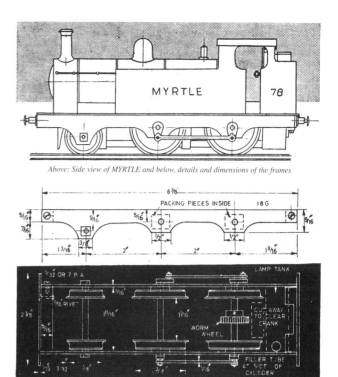

Above: Side view of MYRTLE and below, details and dimensions of the frames

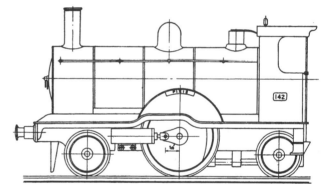

sighted; and that he always called an injector an 'inspirator'.

By the way, when at the Paris Exhibition of 1889, he was informed that his engine *Edward Blount* (Gladstone class) would have got the top award if he had had any means of feeding the boiler while standing still; she had only the usual crosshead pumps. His reply was that his engines were built for *running*, not standing still - hence the chuckle when he spoke of the 'inspirator.'

I'm not interested in Spiritualism but certain well-known folk are quite convinced that the spirit of the great locomotive engineer actually did come from the Great Beyond that night to advise me on the job.

So on this happy note - *Grosvenor* turned out to be everything her two creators could have hoped for - this account of Curly's career as a writer, now almost over, comes to a stop.

MYRTLE was a beginners' 'quickie' design briefly featured in the Model Engineer in 1955.

PIXIE (above) and ROSE (below) were two small beginners' designs for 2½in and 1 gauge respectively which appeared in the Model Engineer during 1957. The latter was a small version of PETROLEA - the example illustrated was built by David Street.

Although his eightieth ('official') birthday was now approaching, Curly remained bitter about his enforced retirement, in spite of letters from all over the world expressing support, sympathy and continued admiration. The Otago Model Engineering Society, 12,000 miles away in far-off New Zealand and the Circulo Curly des Aficionados a le Mecanica en Minatura of Buenos Aires were the most distant of the clubs that elected him as patron, president or honorary members. Novelist Neville Shute made someone like Curly the hero of his best-seller 'Trustee from the Toolroom', first published in 1960, and this was a kind of recognition that comes to few. In the book it was Keith Stewart rather than Lillian Lawrence as it was just after World War II rather than World War I that the former took up writing full-time on model engineering. The story relates how Stewart used the Old Train Network to fly free of charge to Honolulu and then sail hundreds of miles to recover his little niece's (Curly had a niece he was very fond of too) inheritance of diamonds from a remote Pacific island where her parents' small yacht had been wrecked. Apart from flying, one easily imagines it all happening to Curly when *he* was in his forties. The network of admirers from millionaires to miners, living all over the world, was completely authentic. The plot, could, of course, apply to other long-term contributors to the M.E.

Another book published around this time had much relevance to Curly's condition; this was called *Roberta Cowell - An Autobiography*. Robert Cowell, ex-fighter pilot, ex-prisoner-of-war, ex-racing motorist, was fortunate enough to be, first, young and reasonably well-to-do, and second, in no way a public figure when he decided to acknowledge his instinctively felt femininity by seeking medical treatment. This involved a two year course of taking female hormones followed by surgery, both abdominal and facial; thus going a good deal further than Curly did. In the end Roberta Cowell settled down with content to the life of a woman, achieving legal and social acceptance; this included an endorsement on her birth certificate, something that Lillian Lawrence would not have needed to arrange. Incidentally, Cowell found that as Robert, his natural inclination was to wear clothes like a ragman's horse (he was once just deciding whether to tip a lorry driver who had given him a lift, when the man handed him

POLLY O' FLYNN was the largest locomotive Curly ever made, she was a 'Britannia' 4-6-2 3½in gauge but fitted with outside Stephenson's valve gear and various other modifications. She is now owned by Richard Nixon who is seen attending to the fire.

half-a-crown for his next meal!), but as Roberta, always dressed in the most fastidious and elegant style.

It is on record that Curly himself recognised the parallel between Cowell's case and his own, as an interesting letter received from a friend and fellow freemason indicates. This was G. A. Flanagan, a remarkable man who took up model engineering at the age of 75 and then spent 20 enjoyable active years involved in it. Rather surprisingly because of his strong feeling of feminine identity Curly had clearly been worried about losing his membership of what must surely be one of the ultimate in masculine fraternities, but 'Flan' wrote to re-assure him.....

30-3-54

Dear Curly,

With further reference to your letter dated 20th March; I gave myself the pleasure of an interview with the Assistant Secretary of the Grand Lodge of England, with whom I discussed the hypothetical case of 'Bob' Cowell.

At the same time I put out a feeler as to what might happen to any other individual who might find himself inadvertently included in the same state of circumstances.

The answer is that once a man is made a Freemason he remains as such for all time, unless he should commit some very grievous act for which he could be expelled from the Brotherhood. In the case of Cowell or other similar case, there has been no misdemeanour and therefore any Brother who may find himself in such a position is free to consider himself as still being in every sense a Freemason. Further he is entitled to attend his Lodge always provided that he does so properly dressed in accordance with the regulations contained in the summons.

DILYS for 3½in gauge was based on the GWR 'Dukedog' 4-4-0s, but has a 'Bulldog' instead of a 'Duke' smokebox. She is now owned by Bobby Jones; the driver is his wife Jackie.

Finally it is felt that good sense would prevail in regard to actual attendance at Lodge, but the important fact is that any Freemason who finds himself in circumstances similar to those which now apply to Cowell is still entitled to consider himself as a member of the Fraternity.

Yours sincerely and fraternally,

(signed) Flan

Curly now had time to devote more effort to locomotive building and this time - since he was able to live on his savings plus royalties from the sale of his books and plans - this output was for himself alone. It must be said that the locomotives built in his last years were characterised by a certain quaintness; one feels that it was now a case of indulging a few fads and fancies rather than setting signposts to the future. So neither *Lillie* or *Queen Mabel* ever got built; instead we find such oddities as *Rola, Polly O'Flynn* and *Dilys*, whose never-never land qualities were whimsical rather than significant. For example, *Rola*, whilst a good runner (as her present owner Bobby Jones will confirm) is a rather awful caricature of what was almost the least successful of all Great Western locomotives, Mather, Dixon & Co's. *Ajax* of 1838, with amazing 10ft. diameter solid disc

EVENING STAR was the subject of 'L.B.S.C's' first come-back in 1963, in Practical Mechanics. The construction series was cut short halfway through the making of the boiler. Even so, many were completed.

wheels. Curly's modernisation and adaptation from broad to narrow gauge did not improve her proportions.

Curly's public had always expressed a strong preference for designs of actual rather than imaginary or partly imaginary locomotives; the antithesis of *Rola*, if you like. Thus it is nice to report that in 1960 yet another editor sought Curly out and contracted for a monthly serial describing one of the best and most famous real locomotives ever. This was the 2-10-0 *Evening Star*, the last steam locomotive built by or for British Railways - if one excepts the *Sans Pareil* replica of 1980 and a few small 'foreigners' (of LBSC design!) built in diesel workshops. The editor was A. T. Collins and the magazine Newnes' Practical Mechanics and with a whole month between instalments. Curly had time to do a super job. Listen to him in December 1962 at the end of the 22nd instalment, describing how to braze the crownstays to the firebox wrapper sheet. Do many people write so clearly at the age of 80?

The next brazing job

Smear some wet flux all around the joint between barrel and tubeplate flange, around the tube ends, and along the four crownstay flanges. Get a tray of some sort about 1ft. square or round - the lid of a biscuit tin would do - and cut a hole in it 4¾in. dia. to fit over the boiler barrel. Stand the boiler on end, and put the tray over it, about 3in. from the top, propping it up with a couple of bricks, or something similar, to prevent it from slipping down while the job is under way. Pile some small coke or breeze in the tray, all around the barrel, to the level of the tubeplate, and get the blowlamp going good and strong.

Use either easy-running brazing-strip or coarse-grade silver-solder for the circumferential joint. Play the flame all over the tubeplate and barrel end until they are well heated, then concentrate on that part of the joint farthest away from the tubes. As soon as it glows bright red - the coke will help - apply the strip and when it melts and flows in, work your way steadily right around the barrel, directing the flame partly inside and partly outside, until you get a nice even fillet between barrel and tubeplate. Next direct the flame on the tube ends (watch your step here, to avoid burning them) and when they and the surrounding metal become medium red, apply a strip of best-grade silver-solder, or Easyflo, to each. As this melts at low temperature it will 'flash' around each tube, filling the countersink and making a perfect seal.

Now some quick action is called for. Take the tray off the barrel, grip the boiler with the big tongs, holding by the throatplate - mind it doesn't slip! - and lay it in the brazing pan with the firebox overhanging the edge (see sketch). Put a brick or something else fairly heavy on the barrel, to prevent the whole issue from tipping over. Play the blowlamp flame on the firebox wrapper from the underneath, until it glows red. Then feed in a strip of each crownstay flange, and keep the heat on until the melted metal has sweated full length between flanges and wrapper.

If possible, enlist the services of an assistant with another blowlamp (2½-pint size would do) on this job. The assistant should play the flame on the outside of the wrapper, while the operator directs his flame on the inside, along the flanges. Literally caught between two fires, the metal will rapidly heat to the required temperature, and the silver-solder will melt and penetrate in fine style, sealing all the rivets. When the redness dies away, put the boiler in the pickle bath again, but stand well clear of the splashes and fumes. What I do is to use the tongs to stand the hot

ROLA was built by Curly for a whim; the basis was the early GWR 'Ajax' with 10ft. dia. disc driving wheels. The small edition is 'modernised' and altered from broad to standard gauge proportions. The model is now in the hands of Bobby Jones.

boiler beside the pickle bath, then get the garden rake to lift it in. The handle of the rake is long enough to enable me to keep a safe distance! Let the job soak for the usual 15 minutes or so, then it can be fished out with the tongs, the acid pickle drained out, and the boiler well washed in running water. Rub up the outside with a handful of steel wool or some scouring powder, ready to handle for the final stage of assembly.

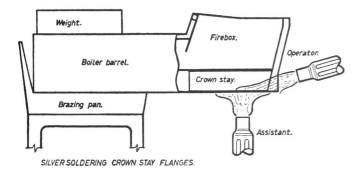

SILVER SOLDERING CROWN STAY FLANGES.

Possibly pressurised by the take-over of Newnes by the Daily Mirror group, one regrets to have to record that at this very critical moment the editor decided that *Practical Mechanics* circulation was not being favourably affected by the *Evening Star* serial; he considered with, I think, some truth that readers of this particular magazine tended to prefer articles on constructions of the bolt-together kind, rather than those dependant on the lengthy processes of actually working in metals. Anyway, that was the end.

In true Fleet Street tradition the author was blamed publicly for this sudden cut-off; although two further instalments were already in their hands. Of course, Curly threatened them with fire and brimstone and a number of aggrieved builders wrote in, but to no avail. They either had to do their own thing (though Curly helped by correspondence) or wait until the series was completely finished off by Martin Evans in the Model Engineer twelve years later. Incidentally castings, drawings and parts for *Evening Star* are still available from Reeves of Birmingham and other suppliers. One of those who wrote in was Geoffrey Cashmore, one of Curly's few close friends at that time; but in fact Practical Mechanics was nearing the end of the line anyway and was shortly to cease publication. Geoffrey was introduced to Curly by Flan and there was also the fact that his club, the North London Society of Model Engineers, had appointed LBSC their patron. In due time, Geoffrey got into the way of visiting No. 121 Grange Road regularly and the invitations usually included one or two friends or fellow-members.

It must be said that these new visitors had both to be chosen and carefully prepared for what they would find. 'Are they all right', an intensely shy Curly would say. The reason that care was needed lay in the fact that a film of Curly's life would have much better starred Margaret Rutherford rather than David Niven or C. Aubrey Smith. Of course, some gentle young man could be found to portray our hero in his younger days. The party would be welcomed at the door by Curly with his high-pitched voice and Margaret Rutherford dress and manner - unwarned this would be rather a shock. If it was fine, they would choose a locomotive or two out of Curly's 22-strong stable and go up to the Polar Route behind the house and have a run. Otherwise, or later, they were ushered into the famous workshop packed with machine tools but so clean and tidy one could eat one's food from the bench - which is indeed what they did as soon enough Mabel would arrive bearing a magnificent tea complete with cakes and sandwiches. There was always a little jug containing, for Curly alone, the accompaniment for the 'engineman's best friend' - evaporated milk. The reason for his having the taste for this fluid was that, if fresh milk was used for making tea which would stand all day keeping hot on the shelf on the firedoor of a steam locomotive, it tasted rancid long before the shift was over, whereas tinned milk did not.

Everyone sat around on stools, Curly still wearing his famous brown beret. None of his friends ever, ever, saw it come off. The master of the house had his own upholstered stool made specially for him by Inspector Meticulous himself. 'I'll go Pullman' was always his comment - it was almost another bit of the ritual - as they settled down to discuss the best of all subjects until a very late hour, for once he got going Curly found it hard to stop. There was another reason why Geoffrey liked to bring friends and it was that on a one-to-one basis Curly's power of intellect was so strong as to be completely exhausting; spread amongst a pair or trio of 'normal' steam experts (if such a remark is not a contradiction in terms) the load was shared.

More ritual was observed as they left; Mabel would appear from the front room - there was nowhere else for her to sit (unless the kitchen) - and say goodbye. She was more shy than Curly in fact. Curly would come down to the gate and as the visitors drove off he would put his hands to his mouth and a loud, even penetrating, whistle would emerge 'Whooo-ee', something like American locos carry. On one occasion, Geoffrey Cashmore was on the point of departure when Curly came down to admire his new car. Seeing a

radio in it he said, 'take it out - you can't concentrate on the road with that playing at you. We wouldn't be allowed one on the footplate! Nuff Sed!! 'Yes Curly', Geoffrey said meekly, 'I see your point'. Incidentally, Curly's own car, an elderly Morris, always referred to as his 'Gasoline Cart' was something special. Under the bonnet it was like the engineroom of a battleship - gleaming, with little oil cups and feeders here and there, also some complicated devilry on the carburettor which did wonders for its petrol consumption.

Afterwards there would be letters of thanks for the sort of day that those participating would remember all their lives. Curly himself was extremely punctilious in such matters; his diaries are full of entries like 'parcel from.. (Sweets)', followed immediately by another one, 'air-mail to ......'. Geoffrey Cashmore's files are full of cheerful little notes thanking him for small services rendered.

Curly's shyness was part of him; once he and Mabel (who was always referred to as 'Scotty') called at Geoffrey Cashmore's home in North London to hand over a large Locomotive Cyclopaedia for onward transmission. Geoffrey was out, but Mabel was sent to ring the bell; when Peggy Cashmore realised who it was she at once invited them both in. 'He won't come', says Mabel and so Peggy went out to the car and chatted. Curly never forgot this small act of courtesy and ever after always asked after 'your good lady' with typical affection and consideration like the Victorian gentleman he usually was. In fact, he often closed his letters 'Love to Peggy from Mabel and me'.

MABEL for 3½in gauge was Curly's last series, which was incomplete at the time of his death. His own edition was finished, however, and is now in the possession of Bobby Jones, whose wife is seen at the regulator.

He showed similar consideration to a then newly-fledged locomotive writer called Don Young, who now runs a magazine of his own called 'Locomotives Large and Small', as well as a live-steam mail-order business. Don was sent a charming note of welcome when in 1966 his first serial (describing an 02 class 0-4-4T from his native Isle of Wight) began in the Model Engineer.

On the other hand Curly sometimes displayed an unexpected (and wholly unfeminine) crudity such as the occasion on which he announced to Geoffrey Cashmore the joyful news that the Model Engineer wanted him back in the fold.........

Dear Geoff,

The telephone men worked all Thursday in this road and when they came to test ours on Friday morning it was still on the blink, so they worked all Friday as well. They don't work Sats, so I still don't know if all is O.K. but I can make a call from this end and that's something anyway.

Shall be glad to see you and Jack on Friday evg. 26th but shan't expect you if the fog comes down. There are two Mabels to see now, one made of meat and one of metal (L&NWR 619 'Mabel') and between you and me and the gatepost the metal one can run a darn sight faster than the meat one!!

Don't know whether you have heard the news, but Howard & Co. have had it. Laidlaw Dickson's firm have taken over the P.M. & Co. business as from Dec. 1st and the first thing Dickie did was to ask me to resume business in the old original style. The idea is to put the M.E. back as it was in Percival Marshall's time, and get all the old readers back. Naturally I'm backing Dickie 100%. Tell you more next Friday. Spread the glad news.

'The mills of God grind slowly, but they certainly make a darn good job of it'.

All the best to all at 80 A.W. from Mabel (the meat one) and me.

Byby

(Signed) Curly

SWANHILDE was Curly's last creation; she was a 3½in gauge edition of a plain Southern Railway two cylinder 4-6-0, after the style of the 'S15' class, but with Curly's mods. such as a 'Lord Nelson' cab. She was completed the summer before his death.

Laidlaw-Dickson came down to Purley with Martin Evans, who was the new editor of the Model Engineer and they fell for this simple 3½in. gauge London & North Western 'Jumbo' 2-4-0. A serial on building *Mabel* was to be the main theme of the new notes, once one or two preliminaries like an introductory lobby chat (21st January 1966) and some criticism of the then recent *Hackfly* serial design. This was a very original work but with one or two howlers as with all un-built designs - even so, Curly would have done better to leave well alone.

This was beginning of a happy time for LBSC, mitigated less than one might expect by the pains and ills inevitably part of old age. He wrote to friends (in this case to Jack Love in South Africa) in such terms as.....

I've had plenty of letters from all over the place saying the boys are glad I'm back again, and you can bet I'll do my best to serve them. But what a time of life to make a fresh start! By the good rights I ought to be crouching over the fire with a shawl around my shoulders, instead of which I can build and run the locomotives, write and draw, and drive the gas buggy at 55mph in the dark in perfect safety! Physically fit (statistics 40-30-42) only trouble is that I get tired quicker than I used to. The editor of the Nottingham Club news sheet says he reckons that it wasn't only Ayesha who went through the firebath.

All the best,

(signed) Curly

Now that the Model Engineer only appeared twice monthly, an article for each issue was not too exacting, while the locomotives upon which LBSC was then engaged were the ultimate essence of the 19th century and 20th century British steam locomotive respectively. By that I mean they were perfect examples of the simplicity which was the steam locomotive's greatest asset and from which designers always departed at their peril, for complication and the steam locomotive never agreed.

His *Mabel* being described, was an inside-cylinder 2-4-0, already built, running and tested at Purley before the description was written, an arrangement which suited Curly best. *Swanhilde*, the Southern Railway S15 class 4-6-0 under construction, also in 3½in.

gauge, was a simple two-cylinder job with outside Walschaerts valve gear. The steam operations of the railway with the world's greatest suburban electrification were rather looked down upon by the pundits of the other lines, who were given to remarks like 'the Southern's freight train always runs to time'; but in fact the Southern's newer pre-1939 steam locomotives were in the front rank. LBSC had in the past described an S15 for 2½in. gauge in English Mechanics, while Martin Evans was to put forward a 3½in. version in the M.E. in 1977 under the name *Greene King*.

Another factor in the well-being of the occupants of No. 121 Grange Road was the new occupants of No. 123 next door. Policeman Fred Harriott and his wife Mavis and their young son arrived in 1963, after the old lady whom the Lawrences called 'Auntie' moved away. It turned out that Fred was an LBSC fan, although at first he was quite unaware of the identity of one of the two 'old dears' next door. Anyway, the ice was soon broken and Fred, who had been a carpenter before he joined the Force, renewed longitudinals on the Polar Route, while Curly did any mechanical work needed at No. 123. Mavis says that her knives and scissors had never been so sharp, while Purley Loco. Works outshopped one of their 'Young Driver' class of 0-6-0 for Harriott junior. Unsmokey meths-fired *Smokey* was a single-cylinder 2½in. gauge locomotive based on the LMS 4F class. She would do ¾ of a mile on one filling and running powers on the Polar Route were included in the deal. Curly liked Smokey so much (in fact she was mechanically very similar to his first ever proper locomotive LB&SCR 'Jumbo' No. 430) that he made a grown-up's version with two cylinders and coal-fired called *Harriet* for himself, similar to the LMS 4562 design.

As 1966 went on, Curly never missed an issue until 18th November. However, a gap of six weeks from 3rd February to 17th March 1967 was the outward manifestation of what is thought to be Curly's first-ever serious illness. One morning some six weeks before, in December 1966, Mabel came hobbling up the path to No.123 saying 'he's ill, could you come'. Curly was obviously seriously ill and in no state to object to a doctor being sent for - of course, he had no doctor of his own, but what else could you expect of a man who even extracted his own teeth after his own dentist retired in 1950?

The doctor diagnosed pneumonia and Curly was sent to the Mayday hospital in Croydon; by the time he got here and was put on oxygen he was not too ill to insist (in vain) on being sent to the women's ward. On 11th January he discharged himself and came home. In fact, his main need from the hospital service was oxygen. Now Curly, already a customer of the British Oxygen Co., for industrial oxygen, only needed to have them deliver the purer medical variety instead and he was in business. Once home, Mavis nursed him and comforted Mabel. The debt that all we Live Steamers owe to this kind, capable and lovely girl for what she did then and later for the founder of our movement in his time of need, will hardly go into words.

The diaries remain blank over this period (apart from the note about returning from hospital) but on 17th January the first entry appears again - 'put new ribbon in typewriter' but 'very weak'. On 18th he wrote six letters (Morese, Copley, Reeves, Fletcher, Coleman and air-mail to Jitsy). By 28th he was feeling 'a little easier' and even did something in the workshop. The following four days were spent on the drawings and article describing the cylinders for the 5in. gauge version of *Mabel*, published on 17th March.

By the end of the week he ventured out - it was a fine mild day - to fill the signal lamp on the Polar Route and put a new licence in the holder on the Morris. Work was also resumed that week on *Swanhilde's* tender and thus one could say that LBSC was back in business. On 7th February he took Mabel to Purley for shopping; although later in the month there were one or two relapses - a week in bed during March, for example - no Model Engineer issue was missed.

Sunday, 2nd April was the day the last lobby chat was begun, to appear on 19th May. It consisted of a description of the loco fleet, now 23 strong. *Swanhilde* had been completed and work was in progress on a toy stationary steam plant for the owner of *Smokey*; this was to be described in the Autumn. Later in April a donkey pump for *Grosvenor* was made (in four days!) - and fitted.

On 7th May, Curly began a new locomotive - to be an example of his American 'Standard' 4-4-0 *Virginia* - and on 9th ('sunny and warm') he ran *Grosvenor*, the first run recorded on the Polar Route since its owner's illness. On 9th June came the last one, when a completed *Swanhilde* hauled her builder for the first and almost certainly the last time. During the following week work began on *Virginia's* driving wheels, but on 20th June entries cease abruptly with a rather sad note 'laid in bed all evening'. Work was done on some unfinished drawings that week of 'Worsdell cylinder', which never appeared; there followed a gap in contributions of nearly two months before the description of the toy steam plant in the issue of 15th September, while on the 6th October came the last-ever live steam note, describing *Mabel's* regulator, superheater and snifting valve. The latter is described with undiminished clarity....

Snifting vacuum relief valve

All locomotives with slide valves on top of the cylinders, or piston valves, should be provided with a snifting valve, otherwise when running with steam shut off, the pistons will tend to suck ashes down the blastpipe, which naturally does the valves, portfaces and cylinder bores a bit of no good. To make one for this engine, chuck a piece of ⁵⁄₁₆th in. round brass rod in the threejaw, face the end, centre, and drill down about ⅜th in. depth with the No. 40 drill. Open out and bottom with ⁷⁄₃₂in. drill and D-bit to ⁵⁄₁₆in. depth, slightly countersink the end, tap

¼in. x 40 to a full ¼in. depth, and part off at ½in. form the end. Reverse in chuck, turn down ⅛th in. of the other end to ³⁄₁₆th. in dia., remove from chuck and slightly broach the hole at the bottom of the recess to true it up for the ball seat, the ball being rustless steel or phosphor-bronze ⁵⁄₃₂in dia. For the cap, chuck a piece of ⁵⁄₁₆th in. hexagon rod, face, centre, drill down about ⁵⁄₁₆in. in depth with No. 32 drill, turn down ⅛th in. length to ¼in. dia. and screw ¼in. x 40. Part off at ⅛th in. from shoulder. Cut the ⅛th in. pipe attached to the wet header to about 2½in. length, nick the end, press the cap on, silver solder it and assemble as shown.

I usually fit the end of the snifting valve through the bottom of the smokebox just ahead of the saddle, but that can't be done in the present instance, as the bottom of the smokebox forms the top of the steam chest; so drill a ³⁄₁₆th in. hole in the side of the smokebox just above the steam chest cover and about 1 in. from the front. When the superheater is finally erected, the spigot at the end of the snifting valve can be pushed through the hole from the inside, the soft copper ⅛th in. pipe allowing this to be easily done. A smear of plumbers' jointing around the spigot will keep any air from entering.

Finally, Curly's life's work ends like T.S. Eliot's World, 'not with a bang but a whimper' with a prosaic correction to a previous note of this serial describing the construction of a classic locomotive, named with affection after his much-loved wife.

Valve-gear erection tip

In the drawing of the Allan valve-gear for the 3½in. gauge engine there is a mistake in dimensioning the position the spindle which carries the rocker arms. Nothing the matter with the drawing, only the fractional figure, which shows the spindle as being ½in. below the top of the frames. As the piston rod and valve spindle are 1¼in. apart, the latter should line up with the top of the frame when the cylinders are correctly erected and as the rocker shaft is midway between them, the distance between it and the top of the frame should be ⅝th in. as shown in the amended detail sketch reproduced here.

Curly himself, now very weak, was to last just a little longer, and on 5th November he died peacefully in his sleep. Amongst his many 'fads and fancies' (his words) was a belief in reincarnation and he had settled down that night secure in the knowledge that his beloved next-door neighbour's new baby was on its way.

A view of the Polar Route and 121 Grange Road taken from a train on the Brighton line just south of Purley Oaks station. No. 121 is the second from left of the block of four houses alongside the little railway.

Mavis Harriott who nursed Curly through his last illness.

Mabel survived Curly and at first stayed on at No. 121; in 1969 she could not carry on and had to spend some time in a nursing home. Before she returned the Harriotts saw to it that No. 121 was made more habitable for an old and not too agile lady by having (for example) the heating arrangements converted from hand fired solid fuel to something more modern and automatic, as well as obviating any need to go upstairs. But soon afterwards, Mabel found it impossible to live alone; she had again to go and be looked after at a home in Croydon where she died in 1972.

The contents of the workshop and running shed were disposed of, the main consideration being that they should go to good homes rather than being sold to the highest bidder. On the whole this has been achieved; on the occasion, ten years after Curly's death, of the LBSC Rally organised by the North London Society of Model Engineers, 20 out of the 22 locomotives concerned, plus 3 others built by Curly, but which passed out of his possession before his death, were present. Fifteen out of the 23 were run. One of the two missing ones had been stolen from the late Reggie Hank's house in Oxford; this was *Jeanie Deans*.

The estate then passed to the Harriotts, who were named as residuary legatees in Curly's will; they sold No. 121 but incorporated the plot containing the Polar Route into their garden. Mavis Harriott, who was a Curly enthusiast rather than a locomotive one, maintained the line for many years hoping and trying to get local live steam people to make use

of it. Of course, the problem was that the area is well served by live steam tracks; moreover, the little 250 ft. Polar Route with its 17ft. 6in. radius curves was not suitable for large 3½in. gauge locomotives and there was no provision at all for the continuous running of 5in. gauge ones. One only has to cite in comparison the 2200ft. track of the Sussex Model Engineering Society just down the line at Haywards Heath, with its 40ft. minimum radius curves, to see what has happened to the great movement that Curly began; and also why his pioneer line of 40 years ago is no longer in the running. A short straight length is being preserved.

I think most of Curly's admirers would agree that his genius did not lie in his qualities as a designer and builder of small locomotives. He was a good designer and a good builder; and his locomotives went well enough to give their makers ecstasies of pleasure.

As a designer, Curly always kept a little back. For example, when designing valve gears there are key dimensions, such as the length of a return crank that cannot come out to a nice round amount because of the geometry. Yet so often nice round amounts were specified for such dimensions. By doing this beginners were not frightened off; yet Curly must have known that because of it the valve events were not absolutely as good as they might have been. So he achieved two things; first, made things easier for beginners and, second, ensured that the master's product just had an edge on those of his pupils. This, of course, is only right.

When considering Curly as a builder, it must be said that virtually none of the 55 locomotives he built himself would have stood a chance of winning the Championship Cup at the Model Engineer Exhibition. For one thing, he was too impatient to add details - his quicksilver mind ran on too quickly. For another, his locomotives, whilst based on well-known prototypes, often had some major modification - the one that Curly would have made if he had occupied the chair of the Chief Mechanical Engineer in question - and this alone would have disqualified them. The only exception might be his beloved 2-2-2 *Grosvenor* of the 'Look Boys and See Curly's Racehorse' Railway.

But when thinking of him as a teacher, it is quite a different story. His writing had genius quality; no one else had the power to inspire people as he did, to do a difficult thing like carving a complete locomotive out of raw materials and rough castings. His way of leading them by the hand was seductive in the extreme, while the instructions he gave were easy to follow.

One reason for this was that each part to be made was the subject of a separate line drawing, well placed in relation to the text to which it refers. Curly's predecessors tended towards complex general views which beginners had great difficulty in sorting out into their component parts. Curly also, when he wrote for the tyro (as he called a first-timer) was very careful never to over-estimate his readers' knowledge, whilst (it must be said) never under-estimating their intelligence. Put another way, one needed a lot of common savvy as well as persistence to build an LBSC engine, but one could start thinking that a tap was just a thing to draw water from and advice

something to be ashamed of.

A sad contrast to the gaiety and genius of Curly's writing is the embitterment that settled on him so often in his later days. Notwithstanding a degree of fulfilment and success given to very few, he was sensitive to the smallest slight out of all reason; this affected his normally excellent judgement.

Another sad thing is that so much of Curly's wisdom is buried away in back numbers of periodicals, many defunct. Because most of his drawings still exist, a number of complete serials have been reprinted - Tich, Maisie, Virginia, Speedy, Mona and others. This is not so bad as regards actual locomotive building, but so much treasure concerning other matters is effectively lost to the world; at least it will be until (as may well happen) computerised data banks take over the libraries of the world. Then, perhaps, future live steam enthusiasts will be able to make the keyboard enquiry 'LBSC ALL BY'. That this might be practical is indicated by the fact that the result, even in terms of current technology, would be a mere 40 microfiche sheets, instead of a bookcase-full of paper. Incidentally, it is rather strange that all three writer Lawrences, L., D.H., ('Lady Chatterley') and T.E. ('of Arabia') were not only close contemporaries but also all three both rebels and loners.

Like his more famous namesakes and indeed most men of genius, Curly had plenty of fads and fancies. He would write in his notes that he never drank alcohol nor smoked; 'just a personal preference' I have no prejudice against either habit'. Yet, if someone asked permission to smoke at No. 121, he was brusquely told to get out into the garden. 'And as far away from the house as possible' he

MAID OF KENT was based on the Southern Railway L1 class. She was Curly's first main-line design for 5in gauge and became extremely popular.

MINX was the freight-hauling companion to Maid of Kent. *Both designs were published simultaneously in the Model Engineer during 1948.*

added on one occasion when Tom Glazebrook had brought over a distinguished American live-steamer, to whom the rules had not been fully explained.

Incidentally, an absolute rule No. 1 amongst even his greatest friends was that one never called without prior warning, although a then young man called David Treadwell once called (it was in the 1950s) and was pleasantly entertained, perceiving nothing odd about the gender of is host.

An idiosyncrasy was a preference for barter rather than payment. Cyril Grose, who took the pictures for the Live Steam Notes over so many years, was never paid for his superb work; on the other hand he received LBSC boilers for his GWR 2-6-0 and 4-6-0 and no doubt much more in the way of advice and help in the making of the chassis.

Another example of this was Cecil Moore, who presented Curly with a Myford super-seven lathe; in return, Curly gave him his locomotive, *Tishy*, plus, of course, a certain amount of free publicity for Moore's Myford firm.

Curly often did things for people for the pleasure of doing so, rather than as a return for services rendered. John Clancey writes ......

In this story mention is made of Curly's humanity and also of his unbelievable production rate. Maybe the story of how I was 'admitted to the circle' will interest as it involves both these characteristics of the Maestro.

Before the war I had commenced building *Josie*, the O gauge N.Y.C. 'Hudson', and had frames and wheels erected. On my return home, a little 'bent' by Uncle Adolf's fun and games I found that noise such as

that of turning just could not be accepted, so I started to cast about to find someone to machine my cylinder castings for me. I tried several commercial houses but they, all still busy with war work, were not interested. In the end, in desperation, I wrote to LBSC, care of the Model Engineer, asking if he could put me into contact with any person or firm who would be willing to tackle the cylinder, in the understanding that I was, of course, willing to pay for the service.

I don't know how long it took for my letter to get from M.E. to Curly, but by what seemed to be return of post I received a little parcel containing a pair of *Josie* cylinders complete, crossheads and guide bars, valve crossheads, lagging sheets, the lot, finished. All this was accompanied by the most charming letter in which he made me a present of the cylinders and telling me how delighted he was to help (typical Curly wording!) 'a victim of the blood and destruction racket.'

You can probably imagine as a result of this, what my feelings about Curly are, apart from the fact that 'Shop, Shed and Road', and *nothing else at all* produced a bank clerk who could build live steamers!

Many professional railway engineers respected him. Robin Davies, for 14 years a senior member of the mechanical staff of the East African Railways, finishing as No. 3 in the hierarchy and responsible for design, testing, research and standards in relation to all their locomotives, writes:

I started to read LBSC's articles in 1936 while I was still at school. I have always held him in the highest esteem. If there is such a thing as a natural engineer, then he was that. Many of his ideas I used in full size practice'.

SPEEDY, for 5in gauge was based on the GWR 15XX series pannier tanks, with outside cylinders and valve-gear. She appeared in Mechanics during 1950 and the instructions have since been reprinted. This super-detail example is by George Lee of Abersoch, Wales.

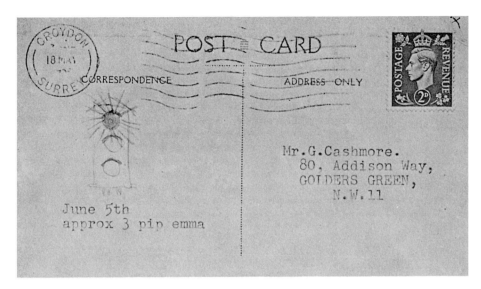

An invitation to visit sent by Curly to Geoffrey Cashmore. The signal, being (naturally) a railway signal shows green at the top.

Even people from other departments found his advice good; for example, at Darlington some years ago there was an 'insoluble' problem of locomotives slipping when starting heavy express trains on the short curve at the end of the down main platform. Because of serious wheel-burns rails had to be changed every few days and this had gone on for years. The curve had been eased at considerable cost (it involved alterations to the platform) with negligible improvement. The only man for miles around to have read 'Curly on Slipping', then made the point that on even a flat curve one wheel must slip; hence only one could 'bite'. He then suggested (to the derision of his colleagues) that the curve should be made *sharper* and hence *shorter*; this could be done so that just ahead of the water column at the spot where the driving wheels always came to rest, the track was dead straight. In desperation this alteration was carried out and Bingo! - no more problem, only a big undeserved boost to the Hollingsworth reputation.

But without any question, the real measure of Curly's success is the great movement which he began. In Britain alone over 100 cities and towns have clubs which own live steam tracks and there are as well many hundreds of 'lone hands'. Similar developments have also taken place across all those far-flung lands settled by English-speaking people; if not quite from Pole to Pole, then certainly from Anchorage, Alaska to Dunedin, New Zealand. On the continent of Europe, live steam is currently spreading like a forest fire, thereby making up for a late start.

In Britain alone, LBSC-style instructions for building small steam locomotives now appear in three periodicals; and only one of these has only a single construction series currently running. At least seven major specialist suppliers cater for the needs of the builders.

On all these tracks, in the catalogues of all these supply houses and in the columns of all these journals, locomotives of Curly's legendary designs still appear with a frequency which tells its own story. And no man could wish for a better memorial than that.

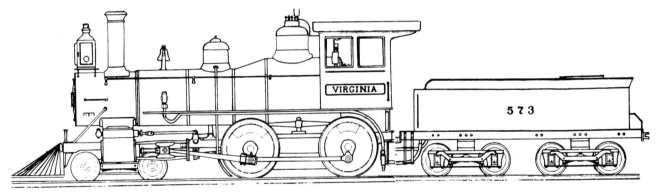

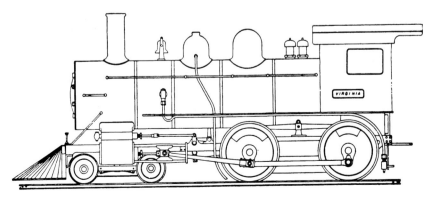

VIRGINIA was a 3½in gauge American Standard 4-4-0 for which the words and music are now offered in book form. There was both an 'old-time' version (shown above) and a 'modern' one (illustrated left). Curly had begun to build himself one a few months before his death.

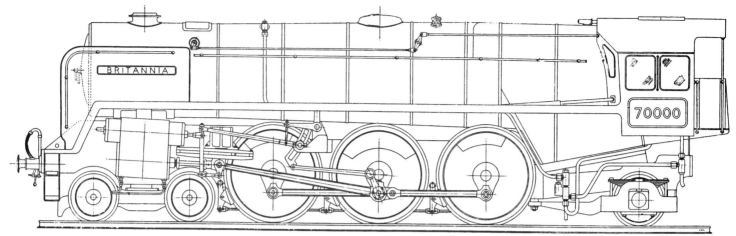

BRITANNIA as she appeared in the Model Engineer on 1st February 1951, the same week that the full-size engine was first shown to the public.

TICH is one of the smallest and best known of Curly's engines. Aimed at beginners, the design is based on that of a typical contractor's works locomotive. Small TICH (shown below) and large TICH appeared in the same series (now a book) beginning in 1948. Curly built his own example of the latter, now owned by Mavis Harriott. As can be seen in the illustration (left) she has outside Stephenson link motion and a matching coal truck.

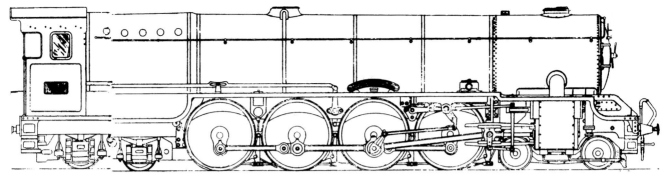

URANUS was based on this idea by Canadian J. A. Joslin for a British-style 4-8-4, brought to life by Curly in English Mechanics. A 'doctored' copy of the drawing was 'leaked' in full-size railway circles and hoaxed a number of locomotive men into believing that such a monster represented forthcoming official policy!

Appendix One

Alphabetical List of Locomotives

LOCOMOTIVES

Published designs shown in heavy type, thus: **MAID OF KENT**
Locomotives of Curly's own build or rebuild starred, thus: GUARISANKA*
Locomotives owned by Curly in 1967 double-starred, thus: ROLA**
Rebuilds shewn in brackets, thus: (Cock o' the North)

DATES: SOURCES

Where a date is given alone, it refers to the year in which a particular locomotive was completed. A contemporary reference will usually be found in the 'Model Engineer'.

Where a date follows letters in this column, thus ME 1947, or (ME 1947), it indicates the year in which the instructions for building the locomotive in question appeared in the periodical referred to, viz., ME = Model Engineer, EM = English Mechanics or Mechanics, MM = Model Maker (British), M = Modelmaker (U.S.), PM = Practical Mechanics, WM = Wonderful Models, MRL = Models, Railways and Locomotives. In cases where the instructions have been collected in book form, this is indicated.

In some cases a locomotive was also built some years before (or after) it was described; both dates are given viz., 1922 (EM 1931) means that the loco concerned was completed in 1922, while the construction serial began in English Mechanics in 1931. Where exact dates are not known, the notation (for example) '1930s' is used, meaning 'during the 1930s'. Availability of drawings, castings and parts from the two principal suppliers is indicated following the semi-colon; **R** = Reeves 2000, (Anker Towbars) of Appleby Hill, Austrey, Warwickshire CV9 3ER; **K** = G.L.R. Distributors Ltd. Unit C1, Geddings Road, Hoddesdon, Herts EN11 0NT. r means that Reeves can supply some parts or drawings.

LOCOMOTIVE	TYPE	GAUGES	DATES;SOURCES	DESCRIPTION	ILLUSTRATION
AJAX*	2-2-0	2½	1890s (ME 1947)	Curly's first locomotive	3, 72
ALYS LOPER*	2-6-0	2½	1938	G. W. style	48, 51
AMY	4-4-2	0	ME 1931	Gauge 1 version of Ayesha	-
				73	
Ancient Lights - see Flying Horse					
(Annabel) **	2-6-6-4	2½	1938	Norfolk & Western Mallet	48, 51
ANNIE BODDIE	4-4-0	2½	ME 1933	Midland Rly style	36
Anticipator - see Charles Rous-Marten					73
AUSTERE ADA	2-8-0	2½	ME 1943; **K, r**	W. D. Austerity	69
**AYESHA **	4-4-2	2½	1922 (EM 1930)	L B & S C R Atlantic	iv, 14, 47, 60
BANTAM COCK	2-6-2	3½	EM 1945; **R**	LNER V4 class	74
BAT	4-4-0	0	ME 1939; **K**	S R Schools class style	59
BELLE STROUDLEY	2-2-2	2½	ME 1932	L B & S C R single modernised	35
BETTY*	2-6-2	3½	1956 (MM 1957) book; **R**	S R Maunsell style	81
BEYER GARRATT (I)	0-4+4-0	0	ME 1958	Freelance	83
BEYER GARRATT (II)	4-6-0+0-6-4	0	ME 1958	Freelance	83
(Black Bess *)	4-6-0	2½	1927	(L N W R 'Experiment' style with (Claughton boiler	22

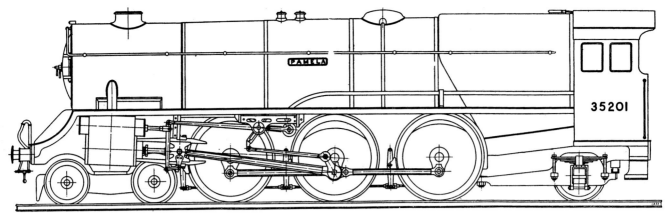

The PAMELA design anticipated Ron Jarvis' rebuild of Bulleid's controversial 'Merchant Navy' class pacifics. She was offered for 3½ gauge in the Model Engineer for 1950.

LOCOMOTIVE	TYPE	GAUGES	DATES; SOURCES	DESCRIPTION	ILLUSTRATION
BLUEBELL *	4-4-2	2½	1932	G E R style (described 1938)	36
BRITANNIA	4-6-2	3½	ME 1951; **R K**	B R class 7	78, 178
B R 75000	4-6-0	3½	EM 1956; **R**	B R class 4	84
(Caledonian 769)	4-4-0	3½	1940		
	Rebuild of Carson loco	62			
CANADIAN SWITCHER	0-6-0	2½	ME 1929	CN style, British option	26
CANTERBURY LAMB	0-4-0	3½	ME 1952; **R**	Canterbury & Whitstable	80
CATERPILLAR *	4-12-2	2½	1928 (EM 1932); **r**	Based on UP9000class	23,106
(Charles Rous-Marten)*	4-4-4+4	2½	1941	Articulated loco and tender	73
CHINGFORD EXPRESS	0-6-0T	1¾	ME 1944	L N E R (GE) class J 69	68
CLINK-BANG COLLIE *	2-8-0	2½	1926 & 1935	GC ROD type (S R colours)	42
				later rebuilt with G W boiler	
COUNTY OF RUTLAND *	4-4-0	0	1951	G W R County class	59
Cinderella - see LMS 4562					36
(Cock o' the North) **	2-8-2	2½	1945	L N E R style	74
CRACKER	0-4-2T	0	EM 1938	Simple loco	52
Darlington plus Altoona *	4-4-2	2½	1939	Pennsylvania-North Eastern	58
DAIRYMAID	4-4-0	3½	ME 1930	L S W R class D15	31
DAISY DRUMMOND	0-4-4T	1¾	ME 1934	L S W R class M7	38
DIANA	4-6-2	1¾	ME 1950	B R style	76
Diesel outline	0-4-0	0	EM 1936; **r**	Steam-driven!	44
DILYS **	4-4-0	3½	1961	G W style	91
DORIS	4-6-0	3½	ME 1948; **R, K**	L M S Black Five	77
DOT	4-6-0	1¾	ME 1949	L M S Black Five style	76
DUCHESS OF SWINDON	4-8-0	3½	ME 1959	G W style (Unfinished)	85
DYAK *	2-6-0	2½	1935 (ME 1934); **K**	Sarawak Trophy Loco	37
DYAKETTE	2-6-0	1¾	ME 1936	Gauge 1 version of *Dyak*	45
ECONOMARY	2-4-0	2½	EM 1931	G W Metro tank style	-
ECONOMETTE	2-4-0	0	EM 1931	Small version of *Economary*	33
EILEEN *	4-6-4T	1¾	1926	Furness style	19
EVA MAY (Tank)	0-6-0T	5/2½	EM 1933	First 5 in gauge design	39
EVA MAY (Tender)	0-6-0	5/2½	EM 1933	First 5in gauge design	39
EVENING STAR	2-10-0	3½	PM 1963 book; **R**	B R class 9 (unfinished)	92
FAYETTE *	4-6-2	2½	1927 (ME 1928); **K**	American/British	1, 23, 70
FERNANDA **	4-6-2	2½	1935	First piston-valve L B S C Loco	41
FIRS 245	0-6-0	2½	1944 (ME 1944)	Present for Bro. Coopie's son	63, 64
(Flying Horse) *	2-2-2	3½	1945	Old-time style	73
FORD PACIFIC *	4-6-2	1¾	1925 (ME 1925)	American style	19
GER 835 TO THE CITY	0-6-2T	1¾	EM 1934	L N E R N7 class	38
(George the Fifth)	4-4-0	3½	1939	L N W R	55
GIRTON	4-4-0	1¾	EM 1949; **r**	S R Schools class	-
GREEN ARROW	2-6-2	2½	EM 1936; **r**	L N E R V2 class	41
GROSVENOR **	2-2-2	3½	1957	LB & S C R single	78, 87
GUARISANKA *	2-6-0	1	1937	Gauge 1 version of *Dyak*	45
GWEN ELMS	4-6-4	2½	EM 1939; **r**	Combination of Rly companies	57
G W R 1000	4-6-0	3½	EM 1946; **R**	G W R County class	76
G W R 1695	0-6-0ST	2½	EM 1939	G W R saddle tank	58
G W R 5.15 FROM THE CITY	2-6-2T	1¾	EM 1936	G W R 51XX class	38
HARRIET **	0-6-0	2½	1967	L M S class 4F (see L M S 4562)	36
HELEN LONG *	4-8-4T	2½	1926 (ME 1927)	For James Joslin of Toronto	22
Helen Shorter	4-8-0	2½	1930s	Tender version of *Helen Long*	46
HIELAN' LASSIE	4-6-2	3½	ME 1946: **R, K**	L N E R rebuilt A1 Pacific	75

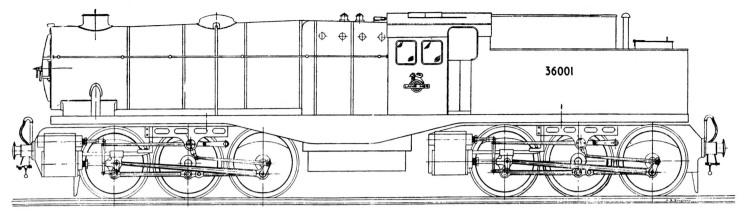

LEADER was a suggestion for a sensible alternative to Oliver Bulleid's amazing sleeve valve 0-6+6-0. Eric Hobday brought her to life with his model 'NUFF SAID'.

LOCOMOTIVE	TYPE	GAUGES	DATES; SOURCES	DESCRIPTION	ILLUSTRATION
Hollywood Annie	4-4-0	2½	ME 1936	Outline only	40
(Iolanthe)	4-4-0	2½	1925	Freelance style	-
IRIS *	0-6-0	3½	1941 (ME 1942); **K**	G W style (Curly's own build was 2½in gauge)	62
IVY HALL	4-6-0	3½	ME 1955; **r**	G W style	79
JEANIE DEANS *	2-4-0	3½	1946; **R**	L N W Webb compound	71
JENNY LIND	2-2-2	3½	EM 1942; **r**	Stephenson 'Patentee'	61
JOSIE *	4-6-4	0	ME 1933; **K**	New York Central Hudson	37
JUDY	4-6-4	2½	ME 1930	New York Central Hudson	30
JULIET *	0-4-0T	3½	ME 1946, **R, K**	Ideal beginner's loco	76
JULIET II	0-4-0T	3½	ME 1952; **R, K**	Ideal beginner's loco	76
KINGETTE	4-6-0	2½	ME 1932	G W R King class	35
(Lady Charlotte)	2-2-2	2½	1942	'A lass of the old brigade'	73
LADY KITTY *	2-8-0	2½	1929 (ME 1929)	G W R 47xx class	25
LADY OF LYONESSE *	4-6-0	2½	1938	G W R style	53
LADY OF NARRANGASSET *	4-2-2	2½	1925	G W R style	18
LB & SCR Stroudley 'D' *	0-4-2T	2 ?	1890s	Early attempt	5
LBSCR	0-4-4T	2½	EM 1935		-
LB & SCR 430 *	0-6-0	2	1900s	LB & SCR 'Jumbo'	
LEADER	0-6-6-0	-	ME 1950	Antidote to Bulleid's SR Leader class	105
LIBERATION	2-8-0	2½	EM 1947	U N R A A design (Vulcan)	84
LICKHAM HALL	4-6-0	3½	Reeves 1956; **R**	G W R Hall class	
LILA	0-6-0T	1	EM 1941; **r**	for beginners	63
Lillie	4-6-2	56½	ME 1955	Sketch only	86
LITTLE JACK HORNER	2-6-2	1¾	ME 1931	Narrow gauge design	33
LMS 2537	2-6-4T	2½	EM 1935	Stainer type	42
LMS 4562	0-6-0	2½	EM 1937	Midland 4F	36
LUCY ANNA	4-8-4	0	M 1935	U.S.A. style	29
LYLIA	0-6-0T	2	MRL 1912	LB & SCR style	10
MABEL **	2-4-0	3½	1960s ME 1966; **R**	LNWR style (unfinished)	94
MABEL HALL	4-6-0	2½	EM 1932	GWR Hall class	34
L&NWR	2-4-2T	2	1910s		-
Magnum Opus or Maggie - see Vindictive					
MAID OF KENT	4-4-0	5	ME 1947; **R, K**	SECR L1 class	98
MAISIE *	4-4-2	3½	ME 1935 book; **R, K**	GN Atlantic	34
MARY ANNE *	0-6-0	2½	ME 1934	LNER J39 class	40
MINNEHAHA *	4-4-2	0	ME 1928	American style	22
MINX	0-6-0	5	ME 1948	LB & SCR class C2x	99
MISS ECONOMY	2-4-0T	1¾	EM 1931	Gauge 1 version of *Economette*	33
MISS HASTY	------	2½	EM 1936	Steam railcar	107
MISS LINDY *	4-4-2	2½	1929	L & YR	26
MISS TEN-TO-EIGHT	4-4-0	3½	ME 1939; **K, r**	NER class R1	56
MISS THERM	0-6-0T	0	ME 1931	Narrow gauge gas-works shunter	33
MOLLY	0-6-0T	3½	ME 1941; **R, K**	LMS Jinty	65
MOLLYETTE	0-6-0T	0	ME 1943	O gauge version of *Molly*	75
MONA **	0-6-2T	2½	MM 1954 book; **R**	LNER style	80
MYRTLE	2-4-0T	0	ME 1956	Simple toy loco	89
NETTA	0-8-0	3½/5	ME 1954; **R**	NER T1 class (LNER Q5)	79
(also in 0, 1¾ & 2½ in gauges)					
NIPPY	2-2-2	2½	EM 1932	LNWR style	36
NORA *	4-6-2T	2½	1922	LB & SCR style	-
NYC 999 *	4-4-0	?	1900s	Set of castings by Drake	-
(Olga) **	4-4-2T	2½	1945	LNW Precursor tank	70

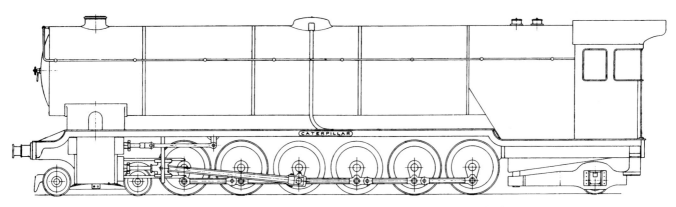

CATERPILLAR - as her designer and builder said 'the result of a bad headache!'

OLYMPIADE	4-6-0	2½	ME 1938; **K**	LMS Jubilee class	54
OWL	0-6-0	0	ME 1940	IMS style	59
PAMELA	4-6-2	3½	ME 1950	SR style	104
PANSY	0-6-0T	5	ME 1958; **R, K**	GWR 57xx pannier tank	86
PETROLEA	2-4-0	3½	ME 1943; **K**	GER class T19	69
PIXIE	2-2-2	2½	ME 1957	Similar to *Nippy*	89
(Polly) *	4-2-2	2½	1927	GCR Pollitt single	25
POLLY O' FLYNN **	4-6-2	3½	1959	B R style	90
PRINCESS EVA	4-6-4	0	1942	LMS style version of *Josie*	68 *
PRINCESS MARINA	2-6-0	3½	EM 1935 book; **R**	LMS Stanier mogul 50	
Princess Mary *	4-6-0	2½	1922	GWR Star class	15
PRINCESS ROYAL	4-6-2	2½	EM 1933; **r**	LMS	45
PURLEY GRANGE *	4-6-0	2½	1940 (ME 1937); **K**	GWR Grange class	49
P. V. BAKER	0-6-0T	3½	ME 1945; **K**	Piston valves, Baker gear	72
Queen Mabel	4-6-4	56½	ME 1951	Possible full size loco	86
(Queen Isobel)	4-4-0	2	1927	LNWR style rebuilt as GCR	-
REEVES	0-6-0T	5	1950s; **R**	5 in gauge edition of *Vera*	-
RAINHILL	0-2-2	3½	ME 1941; **K**	Stephenson's *Rocket* style	65
RIVER STYX *	2-6-4T	2	1927	S R River class style	26
ROEDEAN	4-4-0	3½	EM 1948; **R**	S R Schools class	i, front end paper
ROLA **	2-2-2	3½	1960	Based on GWR broad gauge 93	
(Roland Phillips)	4-4-2	3½	1928	G N R type	-
ROSE	2-4-0	2½	ME 1957	Small version of *Petrolea*	89
S15	4-6-0	2½	EM 1938; **r**	S R S15 class	53
Saddle tank	0-4-0T	0	1924		-
ST. HILDA'S	4-4-0	1¾	EM 1931	S R Schools class	-
SIMPLE SALLY *	4-4-0	2½	1926 (ME 1926)	N E R 1619 class	21
SIR MORRIS DE COWLEY **	4-6-2	0	1926 (ME 1926); **K**	S R style	21
SISTER DORA	2-4-0	3½	ME 1932	L N W R Precedent	31
SMALL BASS	0-4-0T	1¾	EM 1930	Narrow gauge industrial shunter	32
SMOKY *	0-6-0	2½	1962	L M S 4F style (see Firs 245)	63, 64
SOUTHERN MAID	0-6-0	2½	ME 1936; **K**	S R style	43
SPEEDY	0-6-0T	5	EM 1950 book; **R**	GW 15XX class	100
SPEEDYETTE	0-6-0T	1¾	EM 1951	Gauge 1 version of *Speedy*	-
SWANHILDE **	4-6-0	3½	1967	S R style	95
(Sybil) **	4-4-0		1949	L N W R Precursor class	64
(Sylvanie) *	4-6-2	2½	1930	Pennsylvania	28
TALULA	4-6-4T	2½	WM 1928	Lancashire & Yorkshire	24
(Tango)	2-8-0	1	1927	G N style, Southern valve gear	27
TICH I	0-4-0T	3½	ME 1949; **R, K**	Small *Tich*	102
TICH II	0-4-0T	3½	ME 1949; **R, K**	Large *Tich*	102
TICH III	0-4-0T	3½	ME 1958	Improved version	102
(a book covers all three versions of Tich)					
(Tiger)	4-4-2	2	1926	G N Atlantic	-
(Tishy) **	4-6-2	2½	1937	L N E R A1 class	52, 60
TITFIELD THUNDERBOLT	0-4-2	5/3½	ME 1953; **R**	Liverpool & Manchester Lion	80
TUGBOAT ANNIE **	4-6-2	2½	1942	S R style, 4-6-2, Holcroft valve gear	66, 67
U.S. AUSTERITY	2-8-0	2½	EM 1943; **r**	U. S. World War II	70
UGLY DUCKLING	0-6-0	2½	ME 1936	Diesel outline	44
URANUS	4-8-4	2½	EM 1932	GWR style	103
VERA	0-6-0T	5	1951; **R**	For A. J. Reeves & Co.	79
VINDICTIVE *	4-6-2	2½	1924	Railway Magazine heading	15, 16
VIRGINIA	4-4-0	3½	ME 1956; **R, K**	Old-time American	101
VIRGINIA (large)	4-4-0	3½	ME 1956; **R, K**	Modern America	101
(a book covers both versions of Virginia)					
WD	2-8-0	1¾	EM 1957; **r**	L M S Stanier type	60
ZOE	2-8-2	1¾/3½	ME 1957	Narrow gauge	88

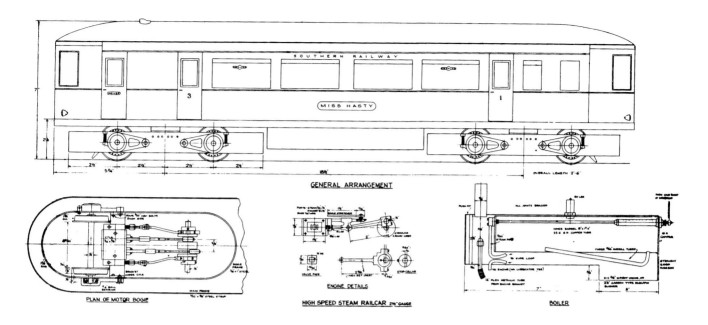

SOUTHERN RAILWAY

MISS HASTY

3

1

GENERAL ARRANGEMENT

PLAN OF MOTOR BOGIE

ENGINE DETAILS

HIGH SPEED STEAM RAILCAR 2½" GAUGE

BOILER

MISS HASTY was an unusual design for a high-speed steam railcar, offered to English Mechanics readers in 1936.

VALVE GEARS from the subject of the back end-papers; they were one of Curly's greatest specialities. The collection depicted here demonstrates his range by showing a miscellany of exotic arrangements offered to readers over the years. Reading from left to right and starting at the top there is first the radial-arm version of Hackworth's gear with the more usual slide-block version (for Owl) *below. Next comes Hackworth arranged horizontally and immediately underneath Southern valve gear - these last two are almost identical.*

To the right again are a pair of gears (Churchwards 'scissors' and Young's) which use the movements of the right-hand main motion to actuate valves on the left-hand side of the locomotive and vice versa. In the top right-hand corner is the GWR Stephenson arrangement (for L B S C's GWR 1000) and, below, its opposite in the form of Gooch's valve gear.

The principal drawings in the lower half are (to the left) the 'gab' motion Titfield Thunderbolt *and Joy's valve gear for* Minx. *Below on the right comes first a sketch shewing the difference between the Greenly and the Heywood straight link valve gear and, finally, in the bottom right-hand corner is Joy gear arranged outside the frames as on the famous Lynton & Barnstaple 2-6-2T engines.*

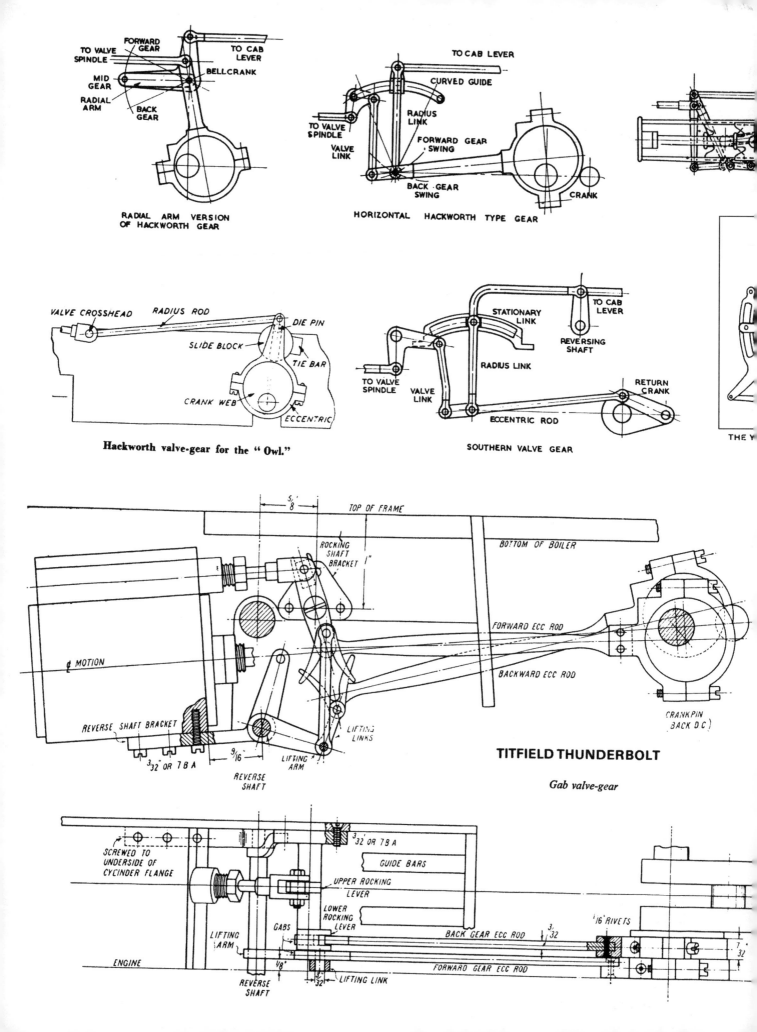

RADIAL ARM VERSION OF HACKWORTH GEAR

TO VALVE SPINDLE · FORWARD GEAR · TO CAB LEVER · BELLCRANK · MID GEAR · RADIAL ARM · BACK GEAR

HORIZONTAL HACKWORTH TYPE GEAR

TO CAB LEVER · CURVED GUIDE · RADIUS LINK · TO VALVE SPINDLE · VALVE LINK · FORWARD GEAR SWING · BACK GEAR SWING · CRANK

Hackworth valve-gear for the "Owl."

VALVE CROSSHEAD · RADIUS ROD · DIE PIN · SLIDE BLOCK · TIE BAR · CRANK WEB · ECCENTRIC

SOUTHERN VALVE GEAR

STATIONARY LINK · TO CAB LEVER · REVERSING SHAFT · RADIUS LINK · TO VALVE SPINDLE · VALVE LINK · RETURN CRANK · ECCENTRIC ROD

THE Y...

TITFIELD THUNDERBOLT

Gab valve-gear

$\frac{5}{8}$ · TOP OF FRAME · BOTTOM OF BOILER · ROCKING SHAFT BRACKET · 1" · FORWARD ECC ROD · ℄ MOTION · BACKWARD ECC ROD · REVERSE SHAFT BRACKET · LIFTING LINKS · CRANKPIN BACK D C) · $\frac{3}{32}$" OR 7 B A · $\frac{9}{16}$" · LIFTING ARM · REVERSE SHAFT

SCREWED TO UNDERSIDE OF CYLINDER FLANGE · $\frac{3}{32}$ OR 7 B A · GUIDE BARS · UPPER ROCKING LEVER · LOWER ROCKING LEVER · BACK GEAR ECC ROD · $\frac{3}{32}$ · $\frac{1}{16}$ RIVETS · $\frac{7}{32}$ · LIFTING ARM · GABS · ENGINE · REVERSE SHAFT · $\frac{1}{8}$" · $\frac{3}{32}$ · LIFTING LINK · FORWARD GEAR ECC ROD